Sunset

Light Cuisine

By the Editors
of Sunset Books
and
Sunset Magazine

Lane Publishing Co.
Menlo Park, California

Research & Text
Cynthia Scheer

Coordinating Editor
Linda J. Selden

Contributing Editor
Cynthia Overbeck Bix

Design
Cynthia Hanson

Illustrations
Susan Jaekel

Photography
Victor Budnik

Photo Stylist
JoAnn Masaoka

The light touch is the right touch

Like a lot of thoughtful people these days, you're probably concerned with staying fit and healthy—and, of course, that means eating healthy, too. If you want to eat right *and* you appreciate truly good food, then light cuisine is the cooking style for you. As you'll see, our light dishes are based on the freshest ingredients; enlivened with a dazzling array of herbs, spices, and flavorings; and offered in imaginative combinations.

We invite you to sample our wide selection of nutritious recipes, from hearty soups to elegant dinner entrées to delicious desserts. With every recipe is all the information you need to plan and prepare healthy meals— the calorie count, a nutritional analysis, even the preparation time. Throughout the book, you'll also find useful information on such light cooking techniques as steaming and barbecuing, as well as a number of tips to help you keep a light touch when you're shopping for food, cooking, or dining out.

Calorie counts and nutritive values for the recipes were calculated primarily from amounts listed in Agriculture Handbook Number 456, *Nutritive Value of American Foods*, a publication of the Agricultural Research Service, United States Department of Agriculture.

We extend special thanks to Frances Feldman for carefully editing the manuscript, and to Kathy Avanzino Barone, Jacqueline Osborn, and Sally Shimizu for their help with the graphics. We're also grateful to The Abacus, House of Today, Rush Cutters, and Williams-Sonoma for their generosity in sharing props for use in our photographs.

Cover: Light eating is a virtue *and* a pleasure when the meal includes Stir-fried Shrimp with Peking Sauce (page 62), refreshing Marinated Asparagus with Sesame (page 33) and fluffy steamed rice. Dessert is a sweet classic—Poached Pears in Ginger-Lemon Syrup (page 104). The whole meal is only about 600 calories per person, from start to finish. Photography by Victor Budnik. Photo styling by JoAnn Masaoka. Food styling by Cynthia Scheer.

Sunset Books
  Editor, David E. Clark
  Managing Editor, Elizabeth L. Hogan

Third printing July 1987

CONTENTS

4
COOKING
LIGHT

·

8
SAVORY
SOUPS

·

20
SALADS &
VEGETABLES

·

40
EGGS &
CHEESE

·

48
FISH &
SHELLFISH

·

64
CHICKEN &
TURKEY

·

84
LEAN &
TRIM MEATS

·

100
LIGHT
DESSERTS

·

111
INDEX

To market, to market . . . Bountiful meals begin with fresh, naturally light ingredients you bring home from the grocer—poultry, seafood, dairy products, eggs, grains, and a cornucopia of fruits and vegetables.

SPECIAL FEATURES

7 Light Menus for All Occasions

17 Crisp Breads—The Perfect Accompaniment

25 Light & Lively Salad Dressings

34 Sandwiches with a Difference

38 In the Spotlight: Vegetarian Main Dishes

56 Fresh-tasting Fish—The Microwave Way

61 Moist & Tender Steamed Fish

76 Steeping—The Gentle Way to Poach Poultry

80 Roasting on the Barbecue—A Flavor Bonus

92 Slimming Sauces

112 Metric Conversion Table

C·O·O·K·I·N·G

Parchment-wrapped shrimp, sesame-coated chicken with grapes, pasta primavera, golden poached pears —sound like too much work to prepare and too many calories? Not so! In fact, just the opposite; these are dishes you can prepare in about an hour—and they're not only amazingly low in calories, but brimming with good nutrition and good taste, too. They're just a few examples of the many irresistible recipes we've compiled for you.

Light cuisine has rapidly become the cooking style of choice for people concerned about healthy eating. Simply stated, the basis of light cuisine is that food should look good, taste good, *and* be good for you. It's a special way of cooking that features fresh ingredients prepared with a minimum of fuss, then offered in sensible-size portions arranged to showcase a pleasing palette of colors, flavors, and textures. At the same time, it's food that's low in calories, nutritionally well balanced, and nourishing—in a word, healthy.

Recipes for Good Health and Good Flavor

The recipes we offer you exemplify all the best qualities of light cuisine. Each one has been specially developed so it's low in calories, cholesterol, sodium, and sugar, yet satisfying and good-tasting. *Plus, every calorie pulls its weight nutritionally.* When there's a choice between two foods, we pick the lower-calorie one that, ounce for ounce, packs the most protein, carbohydrates, and vitamins and minerals.

As you look through our recipes, you'll notice that we recommend a

Take the freshest ingredients, combine their colors, textures, and flavors simply but with flair, offer them in moderate portions, and what do you have? Light cuisine—the new style of cooking for health-conscious people who love good food.

variety of foods, eaten in balance and moderation. Our emphasis is on plenty of fresh fruits and vegetables, lowfat or nonfat dairy products, meat in small quantities, and seafood and poultry. Everything is fresh and fresh-tasting. Because we take the light approach to ingredients whenever possible, you'll find, for example, foods sautéed in reduced amounts of butter, and soups and sauces enriched with lowfat yogurt.

No matter how low the recipe's calorie count, though, the food you prepare has to taste good in order for you to commit to a lighter style of eating. That's why we've chosen our recipes as much for their imaginative and mouth-watering flavors as for their contributions to your good health. Herbs and spices, offered simply or in intriguing combinations, deftly season many of our dishes. Often, familiar ingredients are used in exciting new ways to produce some unexpectedly delicious results.

To help you plan meals, we've included with each of our recipes the preparation and cooking times (usually an hour or less for each dish), as well as the calorie count per serving. We also provide the nutritional content—the amount of protein, carbohydrates, total fat, unsaturated fat, cholesterol, and sodium—of each dish.

Note: If the recipe lists a choice of ingredients, the numbers we give refer to the ingredient listed first. For example, if we ask for butter or margarine, the saturated fat content reflects butter. Margarine would have a lower number.

L·I·G·H·T

What's a Healthy Diet?

The best way to maintain good health is to eat a varied, balanced, low-calorie diet. Eating moderate amounts every day from each of the four basic food groups—meat and meat equivalents, milk and dairy products, fruits and vegetables, and grains and cereals—pretty well assures you of getting a balanced diet. Such a diet satisfies your body's need for essential nutrients—protein, carbohydrates, fats, vitamins, and minerals.

• You need some *protein* every day. This vital building block of the body can come from either animal sources (meat, poultry, fish, eggs, and dairy products) or vegetable sources (rice, legumes, and grains). For a healthy diet, eat animal protein in moderate amounts. Select lean cuts of meat; choose low-calorie poultry and fish often. Make lowfat or nonfat dairy products a regular part of your diet. And try combining some complementary vegetable proteins (such as rice and kidney beans) to create complete vegetable proteins as an alternative to those from animal sources.

• Though *fats* have more calories per ounce than any other kind of food, you'd be in trouble if you tried to eliminate this important source of vitamins and other nutrients. Though you need to consume a little fat every day, it makes sense to keep your intake of butter and other saturated animal fats, which contain cholesterol, to a minimum. Using polyunsaturated fats from plant sources—such as vegetable oils—is a good alternative.

• *Carbohydrates,* an essential energy source, may be in the form of starches (complex) or sugars (simple). Foods that contain complex carbohydrates, such as legumes, whole grains, and some vegetables like potatoes—as well as some fruits and other vegetables that contain simple carbohydrates—are rich sources of vitamins, minerals, and fiber. Refined sugar, another simple carbohydrate, is best used in moderation, since it's high in calories and doesn't provide much in the way of essential nutrients.

• The list of essential *vitamins* and *minerals*—vitamins A, C, D, E, B_{12}, riboflavin, niacin, calcium, iron, to name a few—is a long one. If you eat an otherwise healthy, balanced diet with plenty of fresh fruits, vegetables, and whole grains, you're probably getting an adequate supply.

• *Sodium,* found in salt, is one mineral that many people tend to overuse, and recent research indicates that overuse may contribute to hypertension and other disorders.

Creating Light Cuisine

Light cuisine is simple to create because it doesn't require you to stock up on exotic ingredients or learn complicated new cooking techniques. Rather, it's based on familiar foods, carefully selected for freshness, prepared using familiar techniques, and flavored creatively.

Choosing the best ingredients. As every good cook knows, fine cooking begins with fresh ingredients, and this is especially true of light cuisine. Cooking with a light touch enhances the natural flavor of the food. And with fresh ingredients, you have control over exactly what goes into a dish.

Techniques for cooking light. The best cooking techniques are those that use the least fat. Besides being lower in calories and cholesterol, these methods bring out the natural flavor of the food.

• Most people know that *steaming* is an excellent way to cook vegetables to tender, nutrition-filled perfection. But it's also an ideal fat-free technique for cooking fish and chicken. *Simmering* is another fat-free method, one that infuses food with the flavors of the cooking liquid—wine, perhaps, or broth.

• *Sautéing,* a familiar pan-frying technique, can be light if you use a minimum of fat, as recommended in our recipes, or substitute vegetable oil cooking spray for oil or butter. If you use nonstick pans, you can often sauté with virtually no fat. *Stir-frying,* the Asian relative of sautéing, is another wonderful lowfat method of cooking meat or seafood and vegetables quickly—often as an easy one-pot meal.

• *Grilling* and *broiling* cut calories from meat by allowing unwanted fat to drip away during cooking.

• Finally, *baking* or *roasting* in your oven produces a variety of delicious dishes, from meats to desserts.

Adding flavor without adding calories. Put aside that salt shaker and cream pitcher; foods needn't be heavily salted, or your sauces thick with cream, to taste rich and flavorful. Instead, reach for herbs, spices, lemon or lime, and other naturally light flavor boosters. From pea pods to sole, food gains in flavor when you add a pinch of basil, coriander, parsley, or other herbs. And don't forget the spices —exotic ones such as turmeric and curry, as well as cinnamon, nutmeg, and other traditional favorites. Soups and sauces gain body and flavor from chopped or puréed vegetables, or even yogurt.

Your choices in seasoning and cooking light cuisine are limited only by your imagination— so experiment, and enjoy!

Light, delectable, and simply elegant,
dinner for two features luscious Salmon with Vegetable Crest (page 49),
baked new potatoes, and baby green beans; berries and kiwi fruit are the
sweet conclusion. Total calories per serving? Just 565.

Springtime Dinner for Two
(Pictured on facing page)

Celebrate the bounty of spring with a menu that includes fresh salmon, tender young vegetables, and plump, juicy fruits. Quick and easy to prepare, it makes an elegant presentation at any table. Best of all, the entire menu totals about 565 calories per person.

Salmon with Vegetable Crest (page 49)

Baked New Potato with
Lemon & Parsley

Baby Green Beans

Mixed Strawberries, Raspberries
& Kiwi Fruit

Weekend Supper

Ladle out bowlfuls of hearty chicken-noodle soup, fortified with yogurt for protein; then gather around a crackling fire to enjoy a warming supper. Count on about 500 calories per person.

Chicken-Noodle Yogurt Soup
(page 16)

Cherry Tomatoes

Lightly Buttered, Toasted English
Muffin Halves

Tangerines

Spiced Tea

Summer Salad Refresher

What better time to enjoy a light, cooling meal than when the weather turns warm. Planned around a main-dish salad chock-full of protein-rich tuna and a frozen dessert you make ahead, this menu adds up to about 540 calories per person.

Layered Niçoise Salad (page 28)

Radishes on Ice   Ripe Olives

Fresh Berry Tofulato (page 105)

Iced Tea

LIGHT MENUS FOR ALL OCCASIONS

Planning light meals is fun—it's an inviting challenge to select menus that present pleasing combinations of textures, flavors, and colors, as well as provide the balanced nutrition so essential to good health. Here are some suggestions to get you started.

Steak Barbecue Party

With fare this hearty, your guests will never guess that this entire barbecue dinner adds up to just 535 calories for each person! It's so light that you can toast your good planning with a glass of red wine all around.

Yellow Squash Soup (page 9)

Sweet-Sour Flank Steak (page 85)

Sliced Tomatoes & Fresh Mushrooms
with
Fresh Parsley Chutney (page 25)

Roasted New Potatoes (page 37)

Peach Brûlée (page 103)

Mineral Water   Coffee

Family Favorite

Here's a family dinner you can put together in the time it takes the chicken to bake. It's a symphony of complementary colors, textures, and tastes. And the calorie count per person is only about 560.

Greens with Oranges (page 21)

Chutney-glazed Chicken Thighs
(page 79)

Rice Pilaf with Peas

Red & Green Seedless Grapes

Make-ahead Vegetarian Dinner

Ahead of time, bake the rusks and apples, and assemble the colorful main-dish casserole. Just before dinner, pop the crêpes in the oven and dinner's ready. The calorie count for the entire meal? Just 525 per person.

Baked Spinach Crêpes (page 38)

Steamed Carrots with Parsley &
Grated Orange Rind

Moroccan Sesame Rusks (page 17)

Honey-drizzled Baked Apples

Hot Tea

S·A·V·O·R·Y

Soups, brimming with bright vegetables and nutritious seafood, poultry, or meat, bring together in one pot all the best features of light cuisine. Cooked with little or no fat and thickened with lowfat yogurt or puréed vegetables, our soups draw their rich, satisfying flavors from wholesome root vegetables, their lively accents from savory herbs and spices. With their colorful array of ingredients, they're a delight for the eye as well as the palate.

The soups in this chapter rely on naturally light ingredients—lots of fresh vegetables, fish and shellfish, poultry, and meat in small quantities. In some soups, the vegetables stand alone. Hearty egg-topped Two-Season Maltese Soup (page 12) is an example of a vegetable-rich soup that's substantial and nutritious. Refreshing Garden Gazpacho (page 9), a light and delicious cold soup, also brims with a profusion of fresh vegetables. In other soups, seafood or poultry teams up with vegetables to make hearty, protein-rich offerings.

Light soups particularly depend on subtle but interesting flavor boosts. That's why we've often used chicken broth as a base (it's also very low in calories). Many of our soups are heady with unusual and tempting flavor combinations, such as the orange and anise seeds in Chicken Barley Soup (page 16) and the fresh sage, garlic, and lemon juice in Yellow Squash Soup (page 9).

We've borrowed from many of the world's cuisines—Mexican, Japanese, Chinese, to name a few—to bring you a lively variety of ingredients. Spicy Tomatillo Fish Stew (page 13) owes its flavor to Mexican cookery; delicate

In this chapter, we offer everything from light and tempting first-course soups to hearty, satisfying soups that make a meal. All feature fresh, naturally light ingredients, and all are low in calories, quick to prepare, and full of rich, homemade flavor.

Shrimp Drop Soup (page 15) and hearty, family-style Turkey Hot Pot (page 18) are strongly influenced by Oriental cuisines.

First-course soups. Some of our soups—light and elegant in their simplicity—are perfect meal-openers. Sophisticated Fresh Pea & Pasta Broth (page 10) combines sugar snap peas and capellini in a provocative anise- and ginger-flavored broth that has only 50 calories per serving. Some soups, like zesty Sesame-Ginger Steamed Mussels (page 12), can serve either as a first course or as a whole meal, depending on the serving size.

For a simple lunch or late-night supper, pair one of our first-course soups with a salad or open-faced sandwich. Yogurt-based Mushroom & Vegetable Soup (page 10) makes a good sandwich partner; or try Chicken Barley Soup (page 16) with a fresh green salad.

Soups that make a meal. Other soups in this chapter are satisfying and complete enough to serve as a main course, complemented by crisp raw vegetables and bread sticks, crackers, or one of the crunchy homemade breads on page 17. Chunky Mexican Soup with Condiments (page 15) is a nutritious bowlful of chicken, rice, and vegetables; Lamb-Stuffed Meatball Soup (page 18), a gift from Armenian cookery, is rich with ground lamb.

Preparing light soups. Though you might think that only many hours on the stove could produce soups with such tempting and satisfying flavors, almost all of these recipes can be made in less than an hour. Many have make-ahead features that enable you to prepare them in convenient stages.

S·O·U·P·S

GARDEN GAZPACHO

Preparation time: 30 minutes
Chilling time: 1 hour or more

Calories per serving: 45

2 large tomatoes

1 large cucumber

1 large red or green bell pepper

1 can (2¼ oz.) sliced ripe olives

3 or 4 limes

4 cups regular-strength chicken broth or spicy tomato cocktail

1 clove garlic, minced or pressed

½ cup thinly sliced green onions (including tops)

1 tablespoon minced fresh thyme leaves or 1 teaspoon dry thyme leaves

Liquid hot pepper seasoning

Chock-full of crisp, cool vegetables, gazpacho combines all the virtues of soup and salad. This version can take two forms: made with chicken broth, it's light and mild-tasting; made with nippy tomato cocktail, it has stronger flavor and more substance.

Peel tomatoes and cut in half; squeeze out and discard seeds, remove cores, and chop. Peel cucumber; cut in half lengthwise, scoop out and discard seeds, and chop. Core and seed bell pepper, then chop. Drain olives, discarding liquid. Squeeze enough lime juice to make ¼ cup. Cut remaining lime into wedges; wrap and refrigerate until ready to serve.

In a large bowl or soup tureen, combine tomatoes, cucumber, bell pepper, olives, lime juice, broth, garlic, onions, and thyme. Season to taste with hot pepper seasoning. Stir until well combined. Cover and refrigerate for at least an hour or until next day. Stir well. Serve cold with lime wedges. Makes 8 servings.

Per serving: 3 grams protein, 7 grams carbohydrates, 1 gram total fat, 1 gram unsaturated fat, 7 milligrams cholesterol, 435 milligrams sodium.

YELLOW SQUASH SOUP

Preparation time: 10 minutes
Cooking time: 30 minutes

Calories per serving: 93

5 medium-size crookneck squash or golden zucchini (about 1½ lbs. *total*)

2 tablespoons olive oil

1 large onion, finely chopped

2 cloves garlic, minced or pressed

2 tablespoons chopped fresh sage leaves or 1 teaspoon rubbed sage

⅛ teaspoon white pepper

1 tablespoon tomato paste

4 cups regular-strength chicken broth

2 tablespoons lemon juice

Fresh sage leaves (optional)

The lively taste of sage punctuates this velvety first-course soup. Crookneck squash or golden zucchini provides fresh flavor and—a bonus—essential vitamins A and C. Made with ingredients naturally low in calories, this soup gains body and texture from being puréed.

Trim and discard ends of squash; cut into about ½-inch cubes.

Heat oil in a 3½- to 4-quart pan over medium heat. Add squash, onion, garlic, chopped sage, and pepper. Cook, stirring often, until onion is soft (6 to 8 minutes). Stir in tomato paste and broth.

Bring to a boil; reduce heat, cover, and simmer until squash is very tender (8 to 10 minutes). Whirl soup, about half at a time, in a blender or food processor until smooth. Return soup to pan and stir in lemon juice. Heat until steaming.

Ladle into bowls; garnish each serving with a few sage leaves, if desired. Makes 6 servings.

Per serving: 4 grams protein, 10 grams carbohydrates, 5 grams total fat, 4 grams unsaturated fat, 9 milligrams cholesterol, 487 milligrams sodium.

MUSHROOM & VEGETABLE SOUP

Preparation time: 25 minutes
Cooking time: About 15 minutes

Calories per serving: 118

2 tablespoons butter or margarine

½ pound mushrooms, thinly sliced

1 medium-size onion, finely chopped

4 cups regular-strength chicken broth

2 medium-size thin-skinned potatoes (about 1 lb. *total*), cut into julienne strips

1 large carrot, cut into julienne strips

1 bay leaf

¼ teaspoon ground red pepper (cayenne)

½ cup plain lowfat yogurt

1 tablespoon cornstarch

1½ cups lightly packed shredded romaine

Lowfat yogurt lends body (without a lot of extra calories) to this warming winter soup. Julienned vegetables add color as well as essential vitamins and minerals. For a garden-fresh touch, sprinkle shredded romaine lettuce into each bowl just before serving.

In a 4½- to 5-quart pan, melt butter over medium-high heat. Add mushrooms and onion; cook, stirring often, until mushroom liquid evaporates and onion is soft (6 to 8 minutes).

Add broth, potatoes, carrot, bay leaf, and red pepper. In a small bowl, blend yogurt and cornstarch; stir into soup.

Bring soup to a boil, stirring constantly. Boil gently, uncovered, until potatoes and carrots are tender (about 5 minutes). Ladle into bowls and add shredded romaine to each serving. Makes 6 servings.

Per serving: 5 grams protein, 15 grams carbohydrates, 4 grams total fat, 2 grams unsaturated fat, 23 milligrams cholesterol, 554 milligrams sodium.

FRESH PEA & PASTA BROTH

Preparation time: 10 minutes
Cooking time: 10 minutes

Calories per serving: 50

¼ pound sugar snap peas or Chinese pea pods (snow or sugar peas), ends and strings removed

1 large can (49½ oz.) regular-strength chicken broth

2 whole star anise; or ¼ teaspoon crushed anise seeds and 2 cinnamon sticks (*each* 2 inches long)

¾ teaspoon grated fresh ginger

1 ounce thin pasta strands, such as capellini or vermicelli

In this ultralight broth, crunchy emerald sugar snap peas share the spotlight with slender strands of pasta; star anise and ginger provide a subtle but exotic backdrop. This soup goes together in minutes and is a perfect opener for almost any meal. If you can't find sugar snap peas, substitute Chinese pea pods.

Cut peas diagonally into ¼- to ½-inch-wide slices. Set aside.

Combine broth, star anise, and ginger in a 4- to 5-quart pan. Bring to a boil over high heat. Add pasta; return to a boil and cook, uncovered, just until pasta is tender to bite (about 3 minutes). Add peas; return to a boil. Remove whole spices, then serve immediately. Makes 6 servings.

Per serving: 5 grams protein, 7 grams carbohydrates, 0 grams total fat, 0 grams unsaturated fat, 14 milligrams cholesterol, 767 milligrams sodium.

A light and fragrant wine broth,
delicately seasoned with Oriental spices, lends distinctive
flavor—but few calories—to Sesame-Ginger Steamed Mussels (page 12).
Crunchy bread sticks are the perfect accompaniment.

TWO-SEASON MALTESE SOUP

Preparation time: 15 minutes
Cooking time: 35 minutes

Calories per serving: 179

2	cups chopped cabbage or parsnips
2	cups chopped zucchini or cauliflower
2	cups *each* chopped romaine and spinach leaves
1	cup chopped green beans or kohlrabi
1/3	cup chopped green bell pepper or celery
2	tablespoons butter or margarine
1	small onion, minced
1	clove garlic, minced or pressed
3	cups regular-strength chicken broth
4	eggs

From Malta comes this vegetable soup with a double identity. In summer, make it with fresh garden greens; in winter, choose hardy, robust vegetables. Either way, you crack eggs into a tureenful of the hot soup, then bake them in the oven for a low-calorie but protein-rich main dish.

In a food processor, separately whirl cabbage, zucchini, romaine, spinach, beans, and bell pepper until each is coarsely puréed.

In a 3- to 4-quart pan, melt butter over medium-high heat. Add cabbage, zucchini, beans, bell pepper, onion, and garlic. Cook, stirring often, until vegetables begin to brown (about 15 minutes). Add broth and bring to a boil, stirring constantly. Add romaine and spinach; return to a boil.

Pour soup into a 3- to 4-quart oven-proof soup tureen or deep casserole. Break eggs onto surface of soup. Bake, uncovered, in a 350° oven until whites are firm and yolks are soft when touched (about 15 minutes). Makes 4 servings.

Per serving: 10 grams protein, 10 grams carbohydrates, 12 grams total fat, 5 grams unsaturated fat, 274 milligrams cholesterol, 292 milligrams sodium.

SESAME-GINGER STEAMED MUSSELS
(Pictured on page 11)

Preparation time: 25 minutes
Cooking time: About 15 minutes

Calories per serving: 354

2	tablespoons sesame oil
1½	tablespoons minced fresh ginger
3	cloves garlic, minced or pressed
2	green onions (including tops), minced
1	tablespoon soy sauce
1	cup dry white wine or water
1	cup regular-strength chicken broth
2	pounds mussels
1	tablespoon *each* cornstarch and water
1/4	cup chopped fresh cilantro (coriander)
	Green onion fans (optional)

Mussels are infused with the flavors of Asia when you steam them in this heady but very light wine broth. Hearty servings make a meal; smaller portions make an irresistible first course (the recipe is enough for 6 first-course offerings). Good complements are iced radishes and crisp bread sticks.

In a 4- to 5-quart pan, combine oil, ginger, and garlic; place over medium-high heat and cook, stirring, for 1 minute. Remove from heat; add minced onions, soy sauce, wine, and broth.

Scrub mussels with a stiff brush under cold running water; pull out and discard hairlike beard. Add mussels to broth mixture, cover, and bring to a boil. Reduce heat and simmer until mussels open (3 to 6 min-

utes). With a slotted spoon, transfer mussels to a large serving bowl, discarding any unopened shells; keep warm.

Combine cornstarch and water and stir into broth mixture. Bring to a boil over high heat, stirring; mix in cilantro. Pour over mussels and garnish with onion fans, if desired. Makes 3 servings.

Per serving: 40 grams protein, 15 grams carbohydrates, 14 grams total fat, 7 grams unsaturated fat, 156 milligrams cholesterol, 1050 milligrams sodium.

TOMATILLO FISH STEW

Preparation time: 20 minutes
Cooking time: About 20 minutes

Calories per serving: 240

1¼ pounds tomatillos, husked

1 fresh hot green or yellow chile (about 2½ inches long)

1 tablespoon olive oil or salad oil

1 small onion, finely chopped

1 cup corn cut from cob or thawed frozen corn

3 cups regular-strength chicken broth

½ cup slightly sweet white wine, such as Gewürztraminer or Chenin Blanc

1 pound boneless sea bass or other firm-textured white fish, such as lingcod or halibut, cut into bite-size pieces

½ cup chopped parsley

Nasturtium blossoms, well washed (optional)

Crown this spirited fish stew with fresh nasturtium blossoms and serve it, hot or cold, as a show-stopping main-dish offering. Its refreshingly tart flavor comes from the papery-husked green tomatoes called tomatillos; look for them in specialty supermarkets or where Mexican foods are sold.

Rinse and core tomatillos; thinly slice 3 of them and set aside. Chop remaining tomatillos. Thinly slice chile, discarding stem.

Heat oil in a 5- to 6-quart pan over medium-high heat; add chopped tomatillos, chile, onion, and corn. Cook, stirring occasionally, until mixture begins to brown on pan bottom (12 to 15 minutes). Add broth and wine; cover and bring to a boil over high heat. Add fish and sliced tomatillos. Remove from heat, cover, and let stand just until fish is opaque in center (1 to 2 minutes).

Serve hot, stirring in parsley before serving. Or let cool; cover, refrigerate until cold or until next day, and serve cold, adding parsley just before serving. Garnish with nasturtium blossoms, if desired. Makes 4 servings.

Per serving: 28 grams protein, 21 grams carbohydrates, 5 grams total fat, 3 grams unsaturated fat, 11 milligrams cholesterol, 632 milligrams sodium.

LIGHT TOUCHES: THE LOWDOWN ON MILK PRODUCTS

It's true—milk *is* good for you! It supplies calcium and complete protein, both essential to your good health. But milk products can also be high in fat; the calorie count is an indicator of fat content. To help you choose what form you should use, we've compiled this chart of various milk products, showing the relative caloric values in 1 cup of each.

Calories per cup:	
88	Nonfat milk or buttermilk
123	Plain lowfat yogurt
145	Lowfat milk (2%)
152	Plain whole-milk yogurt
159	Whole milk
324	Half-and-half
838	Whipping cream

Natural lightness is a hallmark
of many Oriental dishes, and our delicate Shrimp Drop Soup (facing page)
is no exception. Bright with shrimp dumplings and green peas, it's a perfect
first-course soup.

SHRIMP DROP SOUP
(Pictured facing page)

Preparation time: 20 minutes
Cooking time: 15 minutes

Calories per serving: 100

	Shrimp Mixture (recipe follows)
1	large can (49½ oz.) regular-strength chicken broth
1	tablespoon soy sauce
1½	cups lightly packed shredded napa cabbage
⅓	cup frozen peas

Dotted with tiny pink shrimp dumplings and bright green peas, this light Oriental-style soup makes a tempting beginning to a meal.

Prepare Shrimp Mixture.

In a 3- to 4-quart pan, bring broth to a boil over medium heat. Add soy sauce. Using 2 moistened teaspoons or a small melon-ball cutter to shape balls, drop ½-teaspoon portions of the shrimp mixture into boiling broth. As balls rise to surface, remove with a slotted spoon. (At this point, you may cover and refrigerate shrimp balls and broth separately until next day.)

Just before serving, return broth to a boil. Add cabbage, peas, and shrimp balls. Cook just until cabbage is bright green (1 to 2 minutes). Makes 6 servings.

Shrimp Mixture. Shell and devein ½ pound **raw shrimp.** In a food processor or blender, whirl shrimp until finely ground. Add 6 **water chestnuts,** chopped, 1 **egg white,** 2 teaspoons **soy sauce,** 1 teaspoon **sesame oil,** and a dash of **pepper** and whirl until blended.

Per serving: 14 grams protein, 7 grams carbohydrates, 1 gram total fat, 1 gram unsaturated fat, 71 milligrams cholesterol, 1156 milligrams sodium.

MEXICAN SOUP WITH CONDIMENTS
(Pictured on page 19)

Preparation time: 30 minutes
Cooking time: About 1 hour

Calories per serving: 354

1	tablespoon salad oil
1	large onion, thinly sliced
3	small dried hot red chiles
1½	teaspoons ground cumin
½	teaspoon oregano leaves
1	clove garlic, minced or pressed
8	cups regular-strength chicken broth
1	frying chicken (about 3 lbs.), cut up
2	large carrots
¼	cup long-grain rice
2	medium-size zucchini
	Salt (optional)
	Condiments: Lime wedges, diced tomatoes, homemade (page 92) or bottled salsa, fresh cilantro (coriander) sprigs

¡Está servida! Family or friends know supper's on when they catch a whiff of this hearty, cumin-scented soup. For a lean soup, cook the chicken and broth ahead; chill, then remove the fat.

Heat oil in a 5- to 6-quart pan over medium heat. Add onion (separate into rings), chiles, cumin, and oregano. Cook, stirring often, until onion is soft (6 to 8 minutes). Stir in garlic; then add broth and all chicken except breast pieces. Bring to a boil over high heat; reduce heat, cover, and simmer for 20 minutes.

Slice carrots ¼ inch thick and add to broth mixture along with rice and chicken breasts. Cover and continue simmering until breast meat in thickest portion is no longer pink when slashed (about 15 minutes).

Remove from heat. Lift out chicken pieces; when cool enough to handle, remove and discard skin and bones. Tear meat into bite-size pieces. (At

this point, you may let chicken and broth cool; then cover and refrigerate separately until next day. Lift off and discard solid fat on soup.)

Heat soup, covered, over medium heat until it comes to a simmer. Cut zucchini into ½-inch cubes and add to soup along with chicken. Simmer, uncovered, just until zucchini is bright green and tender-crisp (about 5 minutes). Skim and discard fat, if necessary. Discard chiles. Season to taste with salt, if desired. Ladle soup into bowls and offer condiments to add to each serving. Makes 6 servings.

Per serving: 36 grams protein, 21 grams carbohydrates, 14 grams total fat, 9 grams unsaturated fat, 173 milligrams cholesterol, 1056 milligrams sodium.

CHICKEN BARLEY SOUP

Preparation time: 15 minutes
Cooking time: 45 minutes

Calories per serving: 261

1 tablespoon butter or margarine

1 large onion, thinly sliced and separated into rings

¼ cup pearl barley

⅛ teaspoon anise seeds, coarsely crushed

1 clove garlic, minced or pressed

6 cups regular-strength chicken broth

3 small carrots, sliced ¼ inch thick

1 medium-size orange

2 cups skinned and shredded cooked chicken or turkey

Chopped parsley

Fresh oranges and crushed anise seeds are the surprise ingredients in this familiar old favorite; it's a light but satisfying choice for a main dish. You can make this soup with cooked turkey if you wish, so it's perfect for a post-holiday supper.

In a 3- to 4-quart pan, melt butter over medium heat. Add onion, barley, and anise seeds. Cook, stirring often, until onion is soft (6 to 8 minutes). Stir in garlic; then add broth. Reduce heat, cover, and boil gently until barley is almost tender to bite (about 25 minutes).

Add carrots, cover, and simmer until carrots are just tender (about 10 minutes). Meanwhile, grate enough orange peel to make ¼ teaspoon; set aside. Cut off and discard remaining peel and white membrane from orange. Lift out orange segments and add to soup along with orange peel and chicken. Cover and simmer until chicken is heated through (3 to 5 minutes). Garnish with parsley. Makes 4 servings.

Per serving: 29 grams protein, 23 grams carbohydrates, 6 grams total fat, 2 grams unsaturated fat, 86 milligrams cholesterol, 1184 milligrams sbdium.

CHICKEN-NOODLE YOGURT SOUP

Preparation time: 15 minutes
Cooking time: 45 minutes

Calories per serving: 249

1 tablespoon salad oil

1 large onion, finely chopped

1 teaspoon thyme leaves

¼ teaspoon *each* pepper and dill weed

3 cloves garlic, minced or pressed

8 cups regular-strength chicken broth

4 or 5 parsley sprigs

3 small carrots, thinly sliced

4 ounces medium-wide egg noodles

2 cups skinned and cubed cooked chicken or turkey

1 cup plain lowfat yogurt

1 tablespoon cornstarch

6 green onions (including tops), thinly sliced

A cup of lowfat yogurt adds a pleasant tartness, as well as a protein boost, to this simple but rich-tasting soup. Blending the yogurt with cornstarch before adding it to the hot soup prevents the yogurt from separating. This soup's a great warm-up on chilly winter days.

Heat oil in a 5- to 6-quart pan over medium heat; add chopped onion, thyme, pepper, and dill weed. Cook, stirring often, until onion is soft (6 to 8 minutes). Stir in garlic; then add broth, parsley, and carrots. Bring to a boil; reduce heat, cover, and boil gently until carrots are tender when pierced (12 to 15 minutes).

Discard parsley; increase heat to high and add noodles. Cook, uncovered, until noodles are tender (8 to 10 minutes). Add chicken.

In a medium-size bowl, smoothly blend yogurt and cornstarch. Gradually blend in about 1 cup of the hot broth mixture. Then stir yogurt mixture into soup and cook, stirring, until soup comes to a boil. Garnish with green onion slices. Makes 6 servings.

Per serving: 24 grams protein, 25 grams carbohydrates, 5 grams total fat, 3 grams unsaturated fat, 76 milligrams cholesterol, 1028 milligrams sodium.

The pleasures of baking and eating bread and the pursuit of a low-calorie diet need not be mutually exclusive. As many calorie-counters know, it's not so much the bread that drives up the numbers as it is the butter or jam that's spread over it.

These two crisp and delicious breads—Moroccan Sesame Rusks and Almond Flatbread—taste so good they don't need rich additions. Though it takes time to bake a full batch, both breads will keep for a week or more. Offer either one as an on-the-spot accompaniment to a full-meal soup or salad.

Moroccan Sesame Rusks

These richly flavored rusks are great "dunkers" for coffee or tea, as well as good soup or salad partners.

- ⅔ **cup sesame seeds**
- 2 **eggs**
- ½ **cup sugar**
- 4 **tablespoons butter or margarine, melted**
- 1 **cup water**
- 4 **cups all-purpose flour**
- ½ **teaspoon salt**
- 1 **tablespoon baking powder**

In a wide frying pan, toast sesame seeds over medium heat, shaking pan often, until golden (3 to 5 minutes). Let cool; then whirl in a food processor or blender until finely ground.

In a large bowl, beat eggs, sugar, butter, and water. Mix in sesame seeds, flour, salt, and baking powder. Cover and refrigerate until firm (2 to 3 hours).

Divide dough in half. On a greased 12- by 15-inch baking sheet, shape each portion down length of pan to make 2 flat loaves, each ⅝ inch thick and 2½ inches wide. Bake in a 375° oven until golden (about 20 minutes). Let stand in pan until loaves are cool enough to touch.

With a serrated knife, cut each loaf crosswise into ¼-inch-thick slices. Place slices close together, cut sides down, on baking sheets. Bake in a 350° oven until crisp (20 to 25 minutes). Let cool on wire racks. Store in airtight containers for up to 3 weeks. Makes 10 dozen. *Calories per rusk:* 28.

Almond Flatbread

Toasted almonds give these crisp rounds a wonderful aroma and a distinctive, nutty flavor and crunch.

- 1 **cup unblanched almonds**
- 2 **cups all-purpose flour**
- 1 **tablespoon sugar**
- ½ **teaspoon** *each* **baking soda and salt**
- ⅓ **cup firm butter or margarine**
- ⅔ **cup buttermilk**

Spread almonds in a shallow baking pan and toast in a 350° oven until nuts are crisp and fragrant (8 to 10 minutes). Let cool; then whirl in a food processor or blender until finely ground.

In a large bowl, stir together ground almonds, flour, sugar, baking soda, and salt. Cut in butter until mixture resembles fine crumbs. With a fork, stir in buttermilk until mixture holds together. Shape dough into a ball.

Break off small pieces of dough and roll into 1-inch balls. Roll each out on a floured surface, turning occasionally to prevent sticking, to make paper-thin rounds about 4 inches in diameter.

Place flatbreads slightly apart on large ungreased baking sheets. Bake in a 400° oven until golden brown (6 to 8 minutes). Let cool on wire racks. Store in an airtight container for up to 10 days. Serve at room temperature or reheat and serve warm. Makes about 5 dozen. *Calories per flatbread:* 40.

CRISP BREADS— THE PERFECT ACCOMPANIMENT

Crisp, low-calorie breads are the perfect complement to many soups and salads, especially those you serve as a whole meal. On this page, we offer recipes for two such breads, both so delicious that you can eat them as they are, without topping them with any high-calorie spreads.

TURKEY HOT POT

Preparation time: 30 minutes
Cooking time: 15 minutes

Calories per serving: 331

2 ounces bean threads (cellophane noodles or long rice)

Turkey Meatballs (recipe follows)

2 medium-size carrots, cut diagonally into ⅛-inch slices

6 green onions (including tops), cut into 2-inch lengths

8 fresh shiitake or oyster mushrooms, cut in half if large

6 leaves napa cabbage, cut into 2-inch squares

4 cups regular-strength chicken broth

2 cups water

2 teaspoons soy sauce

A Japanese family meal might center around this whole-meal soup. Look for transparent noodles in Oriental markets.

Place bean threads in a bowl; cover with warm water and let soak for about 30 minutes. Prepare Turkey Meatballs and set aside. On a tray, arrange carrots, onions, mushrooms, and cabbage in separate piles.

In a 4- to 5-quart pan, combine broth, water, and soy sauce. Bring to a boil over high heat. Add meatballs, all at once. Return broth to a boil; reduce heat and simmer for 5 minutes. Skim and discard any foam or small particles that rise to surface.

Drain bean threads, discarding liquid. Without stirring, add to broth, in sequence, carrots, onions, mushrooms, cabbage, and bean threads,

allowing broth to return to a simmer after each addition. (Try to keep each ingredient in its own area of pan for easier serving.)

Cover and simmer until vegetables are just tender when pierced (about 1 minute). Distribute ingredients evenly among individual bowls, then ladle broth over. Makes 4 servings.

Turkey Meatballs. In a medium-size bowl, lightly mix 1 pound **ground turkey,** 1 teaspoon grated **fresh ginger,** 1 tablespoon **cornstarch,** 1 tablespoon **sake** or dry sherry, and ½ teaspoon **salt.** Add 1 **egg,** lightly beaten, and stir until blended. Shape into 1½-inch balls.

Per serving: 42 grams protein, 18 grams carbohydrates, 9 grams total fat, 5 grams unsaturated fat, 178 milligrams cholesterol, 1395 milligrams sodium.

LAMB-STUFFED MEATBALL SOUP

Preparation time: 35 minutes
Cooking time: About 25 minutes

Calories per serving: 295

1½ pounds lean ground lamb

⅓ cup whole wheat flour

1 small onion, finely chopped

1 tablespoon lemon juice

1 teaspoon paprika

⅛ teaspoon ground red pepper (cayenne)

¼ cup finely chopped parsley

¼ teaspoon salt

⅛ teaspoon black pepper

4 cups regular-strength chicken broth

Parsley or mint sprigs

Plain lowfat yogurt (optional)

Kufta—that's the name for the savory Armenian meatballs that go into this soup. A dollop of plain lowfat yogurt will add about 10 calories to each serving.

Remove and reserve ½ cup of the lamb. In large bowl of an electric mixer, combine remaining lamb and flour; beat until smoothly blended. Divide mixture into 12 equal portions; set aside.

Crumble reserved ground lamb into a medium-size nonstick frying pan over medium-high heat. Add onion and cook, stirring often, for 5 minutes. Add lemon juice, paprika, and red pepper; continue to cook, stirring, until onion is soft (about 5 minutes). Remove from heat and stir in chopped parsley, salt, and black pepper.

With moistened hands, firmly pat each portion of the uncooked lamb

mixture into a round patty about 4 inches in diameter. Spoon about 1 tablespoon of the cooked mixture into center of each patty. Bring edges together in center and pinch firmly to seal. Pat into a smooth, flattened ball. Set meatballs in a shallow pan lined with wax paper. (At this point, you may cover and refrigerate meatballs until next day.)

Bring broth to a boil in a 4- to 5-quart pan over high heat. Reduce heat to low and add meatballs. Cover and simmer (if boiled, meatballs may pop open) until meatballs are firm (about 10 minutes). Ladle meatballs and broth into wide bowls. Garnish each serving with a parsley sprig and, if desired, a spoonful of yogurt. Makes 6 servings.

Per serving: 24 grams protein, 8 grams carbohydrates, 19 grams total fat, 7 grams unsaturated fat, 90 milligrams cholesterol, 644 milligrams sodium.

Hearty chicken, rice, and vegetables
are the low-calorie ingredients in spirited Mexican Soup
with Condiments (page 15). Lime wedges, fresh cilantro, salsa, and tomatoes
add that special south-of-the-border touch.

S·A·L·A·D·S &

Crisp lettuce, sunny yellow squash, tender asparagus spears—these and a wealth of other garden-fresh vegetables are naturals when it comes to light, healthy eating. Not only are they low in calories and fats, but they're also rich in essential vitamins and minerals. And their flavors, colors, and textures have endless variety and appeal.

Vegetables are among the most versatile of foods. In this chapter, you'll find dozens of ways to prepare them—from crisp, cold first-course salads to warm and filling main dishes.

Versatile Salads

A salad doesn't have to be simply the familiar bowlful of lettuce and tomatoes, though that can be delicious, too. The salads in this chapter contain a multitude of tempting ingredients —seafood, poultry, meat, pasta, and fruit.

Some of our salads, such as tangy Cilantro Slaw (page 21) and colorful Avocado-stuffed Tomato Salad (page 23), are all-vegetable concoctions. Others, like Layered Niçoise Salad (page 28), combine vegetables with a variety of ingredients, such as pasta, seafood, eggs, or roast beef. Any of these combination salads are nutritious and filling enough for a full meal.

For those times when you want to serve a traditional green salad, we offer an array of inviting light dressings (page 25). Based on such unusual ingredients as cranberries or puréed peppers, these dressings more than make up in flavor what they lack in calorie-laden oil.

What's better for light and healthy eating than versatile vegetables? Use them in a salad, either by themselves or with seafood, poultry, meat, pasta, or fruit. Cook them and serve them up as a side or main dish. You'll find the possibilities are endless —and delicious!

Cooking Vegetables the Light Way

Naturally low in calories yet rich in nutrients, cooked vegetables are basic to light cuisine. The best cooking methods are those that preserve essential vitamins and minerals.

• *Steaming* not only keeps colors bright and flavors fresh but also ensures minimal loss of water-soluble nutrients.

• *Microwaving* might be thought of as a high-tech method of steaming, since vegetables cook in the steam from their own moisture and retain their color and flavor.

• *Stir-frying* produces vegetables with tender-crisp texture and bright color. To keep calories and cholesterol to a minimum, use a nonstick frying pan or wok, add just a little oil, and quickly stir the vegetables in the oil over high heat. To finish cooking, add a tablespoon or more of broth or water, cover the pan, and steam the vegetables until they're done.

• *Baking* and *roasting* are good methods for such vegetables as potatoes, squash, tomato halves, and whole carrots. If you enjoy the crisp skin of a baked potato (that's where lots of nutrients are), mist it lightly with vegetable oil cooking spray before baking. Or try our delectable Roasted New Potatoes (page 37), oven-roasted with onion wedges.

• *Grilling* is another great way to cook certain vegetables. Spray the grill with cooking spray, then add whole green onions or young leeks, red or green cabbage wedges, or halved zucchini.

V·E·G·E·T·A·B·L·E·S

CILANTRO SLAW
(Pictured on page 78)

Preparation time: 20 minutes

Calories per serving: 71

1	**small head green cabbage** (about 1 lb.), finely shredded
1	**small onion**, finely chopped
¼	cup **fresh cilantro** (coriander)
½	cup thinly sliced **radishes**
	Lime-Garlic Dressing (recipe follows)

Light, zesty lime and garlic dressing lends zing to crisp shredded cabbage in this colorful coleslaw. The cabbage is an excellent source of vitamin C.

In a large bowl, combine cabbage, onion, cilantro, and radishes. Prepare Lime-Garlic Dressing and pour over vegetables; mix lightly to coat with dressing. If made ahead, cover and refrigerate for up to 3 hours. Makes 6 servings.

Lime-Garlic Dressing. In a medium-size bowl, combine 2 tablespoons

salad oil, ¼ cup **lime juice**, 1 tablespoon **white wine vinegar**, 2 cloves **garlic**, minced or pressed, ⅛ teaspoon **salt**, and a dash of **pepper**. Whisk until thoroughly blended.

Per serving: 1 gram protein, 7 grams carbohydrates, 5 grams total fat, 4 grams unsaturated fat, 0 milligrams cholesterol, 64 milligrams sodium.

LIGHT TOUCHES: ON THE LOOKOUT FOR UNWANTED SODIUM

If you're eating three meals a day, you're probably getting more sodium —usually in the form of table salt (sodium chloride)—than nutritionists think you need.

If you're concerned about reducing your sodium intake, become a careful label reader. Note the amount of salt in processed foods. Then look for

their low-sodium equivalents; many such products—soups, seasoning sauces, canned vegetables, and packaged cheeses, for example—are now readily available. If you use any reduced-sodium products in our recipes, the sodium total will be lower than that shown in the recipe's nutritional breakdown.

GREENS WITH ORANGES
(Pictured on page 75)

Preparation time: 20 minutes

Calories per serving: 76

1	tablespoon **pine nuts** or slivered almonds
¼	cup **rice wine vinegar**
2	teaspoons **sugar**
1	teaspoon **Worcestershire**
½	teaspoon **dry basil**
2	large **oranges**
6	cups lightly packed bite-size pieces **butter lettuce**
½	cup sliced **radishes**

Oranges supply vitamin C as well as tangy flavor to this salad; the refreshing dressing contains no oil at all, yet tastes so good you'll never miss it!

In a small frying pan, toast nuts over medium heat, shaking pan often, until golden (3 to 5 minutes); let cool.

In a small bowl, stir together vinegar, sugar, Worcestershire, and basil. With a sharp knife, cut away peel and white membrane from oranges. Cut

between inner membranes to remove orange segments.

In a large bowl, combine lettuce, radishes, oranges, nuts, and dressing. Mix gently, then serve immediately. Makes 4 servings.

Per serving: 3 grams protein, 14 grams carbohydrates, 2 grams total fat, 1 gram unsaturated fat, 0 milligrams cholesterol, 27 milligrams sodium.

Plump red tomatoes make appealing
edible containers for light and tangy Avocado-stuffed
Tomato Salad (facing page). Presented on a fluffy lettuce bed, it's an
eye-catching first course or light lunch.

AVOCADO-STUFFED TOMATO SALAD
(Pictured on facing page)

Preparation time: 40 minutes

Calories per serving: 274

4	firm-ripe tomatoes (about 3½ inches in diameter)
2	medium-size avocados
2	tablespoons lime or lemon juice
¼	cup sliced green onions (including tops)
2	tablespoons chopped fresh cilantro (coriander) or parsley
2	teaspoons olive oil or salad oil
	Liquid hot pepper seasoning
	Salt (optional)
	Salad greens

Present tart and tangy avocado salad in bright tomato cups for an applause-winning first course or light lunch. Tempering the richness of the avocado with the lightness of the tomatoes moderates the calorie count.

To peel tomatoes, immerse in boiling water to cover for 30 to 40 seconds; drain. Then immerse in very cold water until cool; drain and peel.

To prepare tomato shells, cut tops off. With a grapefruit knife, hollow out inside, leaving ¼-inch shells. Turn shells over on paper towels to drain. Lift firm flesh from pulp and reserve with tops; discard remainder.

Chop firm flesh and transfer to a bowl. Pit, peel, and dice avocados; add to bowl with lime juice, onions, cilantro, and oil. Mix lightly; season to taste with hot pepper seasoning and, if desired, salt. If made ahead, cover and refrigerate for up to 4 hours; chill tomato shells separately.

To serve, evenly heap avocado mixture into shells. Garnish with salad greens and, if desired, tomato tops. Makes 4 servings.

Per serving: 6 grams protein, 21 grams carbohydrates, 21 grams total fat, 13 grams unsaturated fat, 0 milligrams cholesterol, 14 milligrams sodium.

TOMATO & CUCUMBER SALAD

Preparation time: 15 minutes

Calories per serving: 92

1	large cucumber (about ¾ lb.)
	Chive Dressing (recipe follows)
2	large tomatoes, peeled (see previous recipe) and sliced
½	cup lightly packed fresh basil leaves, finely shredded

Fresh basil, dill, and chives add their distinctive flavors—but next to no calories—to this bright and simple salad of fresh tomatoes and cucumber.

Peel cucumber and cut in half lengthwise. Scoop out and discard seeds; slice cucumber.

Prepare Chive Dressing; add cucumber slices to dressing, mixing lightly to coat. With a slotted spoon, lift out cucumber slices, reserving dressing, and arrange on a platter or on 4 salad plates. Place tomato slices over cucumber. Drizzle dressing over vegetables, then sprinkle with basil. Makes 4 servings.

Chive Dressing. In a large bowl, combine 2 tablespoons **olive oil** or salad oil, 2 tablespoons **white wine vinegar,** 1 teaspoon chopped **fresh chives,** 1½ teaspoons **fresh dill** or ½ teaspoon dill weed, ¼ teaspoon **Worcestershire,** ⅛ teaspoon **salt,** and a dash of **pepper.** Whisk until thoroughly blended.

Per serving: 1 gram protein, 7 grams carbohydrates, 7 grams total fat, 5 grams unsaturated fat, 0 milligrams cholesterol, 111 milligrams sodium.

GREEK PEASANT SALAD

4	cups bite-size pieces curly endive
2	large tomatoes, cut into chunks
1	large green bell pepper, seeded and cut into 1-inch squares
1	cup cucumber slices
1	small red onion, sliced and separated into rings
12	Greek-style olives
	Lemon Dressing (recipe follows)
2	tablespoons crumbled feta cheese

A Greek-style dressing, made with equal parts of lemon juice and oil, contributes light yet robust flavor to this colorful toss of vegetables, olives, and feta cheese. Serve it with grilled lamb or fish, or as a refreshing main dish for a summer lunch.

In a 3- to 4-quart bowl, layer endive, tomatoes, bell pepper, cucumber, onion, and olives, using all of each ingredient for each layer. (At this point, you may cover and refrigerate for up to 4 hours.)

Prepare Lemon Dressing and add to vegetables, mixing lightly to coat with dressing. Sprinkle with cheese and serve immediately. Makes 6 servings.

Lemon Dressing. In a small bowl, combine ¼ cup **olive oil** or salad oil, ¼ cup **lemon juice,** 1 tablespoon coarsely chopped **fresh oregano leaves** or 1 teaspoon dry oregano leaves, 1 clove **garlic,** minced or pressed, ⅛ teaspoon **salt,** and a dash of **pepper.** Whisk until thoroughly blended.

Per serving: 3 grams protein, 9 grams carbohydrates, 13 grams total fat, 9 grams unsaturated fat, 8 milligrams cholesterol, 289 milligrams sodium.

SPRING HARVEST PASTA SALAD

Preparation time: 20 minutes
Cooking time: 20 minutes
Chilling time: 2 hours or more   *Calories per serving:* 179

1	cup cut green beans (1-inch pieces)
2	cups broccoli flowerets
4	ounces decorative pasta, such as fusilli or penne
	Dijon Dressing (recipe follows)
6	medium-size mushrooms, sliced

Lightly blanched vegetables, tossed with pasta in a mustard dressing, bring the fresh taste of spring to your table.

Steam beans, covered, on a rack over boiling water for 5 minutes. Add broccoli, cover, and steam just until vegetables are tender when pierced (about 2 more minutes). Immerse in cold water until cool; drain well. (At this point, you may cover and refrigerate until next day.)

In a 4- to 5-quart pan, cook pasta in 3 to 4 quarts boiling water just until tender to bite (about 12 minutes); drain well. Meanwhile, prepare Dijon Dressing.

In a large bowl, combine pasta and dressing; mix well. Cover and refrigerate for at least 2 hours or until next day, stirring occasionally.

Add cooked vegetables and mushrooms; mix lightly. Makes 6 servings.

Dijon Dressing. In a small bowl, combine 1 tablespoon **Dijon mustard,** ¼ cup *each* chopped **parsley** and **red onion,** 3 tablespoons **white wine vinegar,** and ¼ cup **olive oil** or salad oil. Whisk until thoroughly blended.

Per serving: 5 grams protein, 20 grams carbohydrates, 10 grams total fat, 7 grams unsaturated fat, 0 milligrams cholesterol, 43 milligrams sodium.

Fresh Parsley Chutney

Delicious on tomato or cooked vegetable salads, this assertive dressing is also good as a dip for raw vegetables or as a relish with roasted chicken.

  2 **cups lightly packed parsley (coarse stems removed)**
  ½ **cup lightly packed fresh mint leaves**
  2 **teaspoons chopped fresh ginger or ½ teaspoon ground ginger**
  5 **cloves garlic, coarsely chopped**
  2 **tablespoons lemon juice**
  ¾ **cup plain yogurt**
  ¼ **to ½ teaspoon crushed red pepper**

In a blender or food processor, combine parsley, mint, ginger, garlic, lemon juice, yogurt, and crushed red pepper. Whirl until mixture is finely puréed.

If made ahead, cover and refrigerate for up to a week. Makes about 1 cup. *Calories per serving (1 tablespoon):* 10.

Honey-Poppy Seed Dressing

The honeyed sweetness of this dressing makes it a good complement to green salads that include fruit.

  ¼ **cup honey**
  2 **tablespoons salad oil**
  3 **tablespoons tarragon white wine vinegar**
  1 **tablespoon minced shallot**
  1 **teaspoon poppy seeds**
  2 **teaspoons Dijon mustard**

In a blender or bowl, combine honey, oil, vinegar, shallot, poppy seeds, and mustard. Whirl until mixture is thoroughly combined.

If made ahead, cover and refrigerate until next day; shake or stir well just before serving. Makes about ⅔ cup. *Calories per serving (1 tablespoon):* 47.

LIGHT & LIVELY SALAD DRESSINGS

Salads are a good choice for light eating, but traditional dressings, with their high proportions of calorie-laden oil or mayonnaise, can easily defeat the best intentions. Here we'll show you how you can make delicious salad dressings using reduced amounts of oil— or none at all.

Cranberry Vinaigrette Dressing

Try this tart-sweet dressing, made with puréed cranberries and just a little oil, on cold cooked beets or green beans; or drizzle it over such salad greens as Belgian or curly endive.

  ¼ **cup** *each* **salad oil and red wine vinegar**
  2 **tablespoons Dijon mustard**
  1 **tablespoon sugar**
  ⅓ **cup fresh or frozen cranberries**

In a blender or food processor, combine oil, vinegar, mustard, sugar, and cranberries. Whirl until mixture is smoothly puréed.

If made ahead, cover and refrigerate for up to 3 days. Stir well just before serving. Makes about ¾ cup. *Calories per serving (1 tablespoon):* 48.

Green or Gold Pepper Dressing

Brilliant green or buttercup yellow, this dressing makes do with very little oil. Puréed bell pepper gives it body. Serve it on mixed greens or thinly sliced raw zucchini.

  3 **tablespoons olive oil or salad oil**
  ½ **cup diced, seeded green or yellow bell pepper**
  1 **tablespoon minced shallot**
  ⅛ **teaspoon** *each* **salt and ground red pepper (cayenne)**
  2 **tablespoons white wine vinegar**

In a blender or food processor, combine oil, bell pepper, shallot, salt, and ground pepper. Whirl until mixture is smoothly puréed. (At this point, you may cover and refrigerate until next day.)

Just before serving, thoroughly blend in vinegar. Makes about ⅔ cup. *Calories per serving (1 tablespoon):* 35.

APPLE YOGURT SALAD

Preparation time: 25 minutes

Calories per serving: 99

¼ **cup coarsely chopped walnuts**
⅔ **cup plain yogurt**
1 **tablespoon lemon juice**
¼ **teaspoon ground cinnamon**
1 **tablespoon honey**
2 **large red-skinned apples**
Lettuce leaves

A cinnamon and honey-sweetened yogurt dressing gives this apple salad a uniquely light and tangy taste.

Spread walnuts in a shallow baking pan and toast in a 350° oven until golden (about 8 minutes); let cool slightly.

In a large bowl, stir together yogurt, lemon juice, cinnamon, and honey. Quarter, core, and thinly slice apples. Add apple slices to dressing, mixing gently to coat.

Line individual salad plates or a platter with lettuce. Mound apple slices over lettuce, spooning any remaining dressing over apples. Sprinkle with walnuts. Serve immediately (dressing thins as it stands). Makes 6 servings.

Per serving: 2 grams protein, 16 grams carbohydrates, 4 grams total fat, 3 grams unsaturated fat, 2 milligrams cholesterol, 15 milligrams sodium.

LIGHT TOUCHES: DRESSING SALADS WITH YOGURT

The creamy consistency and refreshing flavor of yogurt make it an ideal dressing for all sorts of salads, from tossed greens to those made with seafood, poultry, or meat. A tablespoon of plain lowfat yogurt accounts for just 8 calories (about 10 calories if it's made from whole milk).

If you find the yogurt too tart, just snip in some fresh herbs, such as chives, mint, basil, or parsley. Or add minced garlic or finely chopped shallots or red onion. You could even try a dollop of horseradish. For color, sprinkle in a pinch of paprika, curry powder, or chili powder.

GREEN PEA SALAD

Preparation time: 15 minutes
Chilling time: 3 hours or more

Calories per serving: 65

⅓ **cup plain lowfat yogurt**
1½ **tablespoons Dijon mustard**
⅛ **teaspoon ground pepper**
1 **package (10 oz.) frozen petite peas, thawed**
1 **hard-cooked egg, chopped**
½ **cup finely chopped red bell pepper**
⅓ **cup thinly sliced green onions (including tops)**
¼ **cup thinly sliced celery**
Lettuce leaves

Put together this light, yogurt-dressed salad ahead of time to let the flavors blend; serve it as a colorful accompaniment to cold roast turkey or poached salmon.

In a 2- to 3-quart bowl, combine yogurt, mustard, and ground pepper; mix until smooth. Add peas, egg, bell pepper, onions, and celery. Mix lightly to coat vegetables with dressing. Cover and refrigerate for at least 3 hours or until next day.

Line a platter or individual plates with lettuce and spoon salad over. Makes 6 servings.

Per serving: 5 grams protein, 9 grams carbohydrates, 2 grams total fat, .75 gram unsaturated fat, 43 milligrams cholesterol, 135 milligrams sodium.

A pinwheel of fresh pineapple slices spirals
out around tender shredded chicken to create refreshing Minted Chicken
& Pineapple Salad (page 32). Intriguing flavor comes from a simple, oil-free
dressing of mild rice vinegar and fresh mint.

LAYERED NIÇOISE SALAD

Preparation time: 45 minutes
Cooking time: 30 minutes

Calories per serving: 353

1 pound small thin-skinned potatoes (1½ inches in diameter), unpeeled

Anchovy Dressing (recipe follows)

1 pound green beans, cut into 1-inch pieces

¼ cup *each* mayonnaise and plain yogurt

1 large can (12½ oz.) tuna packed in water, drained

3 hard-cooked eggs, thinly sliced

8 cups lightly packed bite-size pieces butter lettuce

Layering this classic main-dish salad keeps the ingredients fresh if made ahead; lightly mix just before serving.

Steam potatoes, covered, on a rack over boiling water until tender when pierced (about 20 minutes). Meanwhile, prepare Anchovy Dressing.

Remove potatoes from pan and let stand just until cool enough to touch. Peel, if desired; slice ¼ inch thick into a deep 4- to 5-quart bowl. Add dressing; let potatoes cool.

Steam beans, covered, on a rack over boiling water until bright green and just tender to bite (about 10 minutes). Immediately immerse in ice water until cool, then drain and pat dry.

In a small bowl, blend mayonnaise and yogurt; add to potatoes and mix lightly to coat. Layer beans over potatoes. With a fork, break tuna into bite-size pieces and add in an even layer over beans. Spread eggs over

tuna, then cover with lettuce. If made ahead, cover and refrigerate until next day.

Mix salad and serve immediately. Makes 6 servings.

Anchovy Dressing. In a medium-size bowl, combine ¼ cup **salad oil;** ½ cup *each* **lemon juice** and finely chopped **parsley;** 1 small **red onion,** finely chopped; 3 tablespoons **Dijon mustard;** 1 tablespoon drained **capers;** 4 canned **anchovy fillets,** minced; 1 large clove **garlic,** minced or pressed; ¼ teaspoon **dill weed;** and ⅛ teaspoon **pepper.** Whisk until thoroughly blended.

Per serving: 26 grams protein, 17 grams carbohydrates, 21 grams total fat, 15 grams unsaturated fat, 174 milligrams cholesterol, 290 milligrams sodium.

SEVICHE SALAD

Preparation time: 20 minutes
Chilling time: About 3 hours

Calories per serving: 234

1 pound sole or other lean white-fleshed fish fillets, such as rockcod or snapper

½ cup lime or lemon juice

1 small red onion

⅓ cup fresh cilantro (coriander)

1 small ripe avocado

Romaine lettuce leaves

It's a first course in Mexico, but this lime-flavored fish salad is so good you may want to make a meal of it. Scoop up each delectable morsel with a crisp lettuce spear.

Cut fish into ½-inch cubes. In a medium-size bowl, combine fish and lime juice. Cut 1 or 2 thin slices from onion and separate into rings; reserve for garnish. Finely chop remaining onion and add to fish with cilantro; mix lightly.

Pit, peel, and dice avocado; sprinkle over fish, spooning some of the lime juice over avocado to prevent darkening. Add onion rings.

Cover and refrigerate until fish turns opaque (about 3 hours).

Line individual salad plates with romaine leaves and evenly distribute fish mixture over lettuce. Makes 4 servings.

Per serving: 22 grams protein, 11 grams carbohydrates, 12 grams total fat, 5 grams unsaturated fat, 60 milligrams cholesterol, 84 milligrams sodium.

ASPARAGUS & SHRIMP DIJONNAISE

Preparation time: 15 minutes
Chilling time: 1 hour or more

Calories per serving: 252

¼ cup white wine vinegar

2 tablespoons salad oil

2½ teaspoons Dijon mustard

1 tablespoon chopped fresh dill or 1 teaspoon dill weed

1 medium-size ripe avocado

½ pound small cooked shrimp

16 to 20 cold cooked asparagus spears

⅓ cup plain yogurt

Fresh dill or parsley sprigs

For a touch of elegance, offer this inviting salad of fresh asparagus, avocado, and tiny shrimp in a mustardy yogurt dressing.

In a medium-size bowl, combine vinegar, oil, mustard, and chopped dill; whisk until thoroughly blended. Set aside.

Pit, peel, and dice avocado. In a small bowl, gently mix avocado with half the dressing; set aside. Add shrimp to remaining dressing and mix lightly. Cover and refrigerate avocado and shrimp mixtures for at least 1 hour or for up to 4 hours.

Arrange 4 or 5 asparagus spears on each of 4 dinner plates. Spoon off enough of the dressing from shrimp to moisten asparagus; drizzle over asparagus. Reserve a few shrimp for garnish.

Add avocado mixture and yogurt to remaining shrimp, blending gently. Mound a fourth of the salad mixture beside asparagus on each plate. Garnish with reserved shrimp and dill sprigs. Makes 4 servings.

Per serving: 18 grams protein, 9 grams carbohydrates, 17 grams total fat, 11 grams unsaturated fat, 86 milligrams cholesterol, 133 milligrams sodium.

SHRIMP & JICAMA WITH CHILE VINEGAR

Preparation time: 35 minutes

Calories per serving: 253

Chile Vinegar (recipe follows)

2 cups shredded, peeled jicama (about 9 oz.)

1 pound small cooked shrimp

4 large ripe tomatoes, sliced

4 large tomatillos (about 2 inches in diameter), husked and sliced

Fresh cilantro (coriander) sprigs

Salt (optional)

Enjoy a taste of Mexico with this intriguing main-dish combination of shrimp, tomatillos, and crisp, fruity jicama. The oil-free dressing is hot and full of flavor.

Prepare Chile Vinegar. In separate bowls, mix ⅓ cup of the dressing with jicama and ⅓ cup with shrimp. Reserve remaining dressing.

On each of 4 dinner plates, arrange tomato and tomatillo slices, overlapping them slightly. Mound shredded jicama over or beside tomato slices. Place shrimp over jicama. Spoon remaining dressing over. Garnish with cilantro and season to taste with salt, if desired. Makes 4 servings.

Chile Vinegar. In a small bowl, stir together ⅔ cup **white wine vinegar,** ¼ cup **sugar,** 2 to 3 tablespoons minced, seeded **fresh hot green chile,** and 3 to 4 tablespoons chopped **fresh cilantro** (coriander).

Per serving: 31 grams protein, 30 grams carbohydrates, 2 grams total fat, 0 grams unsaturated fat, 170 milligrams cholesterol, 177 milligrams sodium.

Go ahead and dig in! Tostada Beef Salad
(page 33) combines lean roast beef, onion, lettuce,
and garnishes on a tortilla that's crisply baked instead of fried.
Cilantro Vinaigrette is the light and piquant dressing.

TWO-GRAPE CHICKEN SALAD

Preparation time: 25 minutes
Steeping time: 25 minutes
Chilling time: 30 minutes or more

Calories per serving: 403

2 whole chicken breasts (about 1 lb. *each*), skinned
Tarragon-Lemon Vinaigrette (recipe follows)
Grape or lettuce leaves, rinsed and patted dry
1½ cups *each* seedless green and red grapes

This elegant salad features chicken that has been steeped (see page 76 for more about this light cooking technique). Red and green grapes add sweetness and delicate color.

Cut each chicken breast in half. Place chicken pieces in a single layer in a 4- to 5-quart pan; pour in enough water to cover chicken by about 1 inch. Lift out chicken and set aside. Cover pan and bring water to a boil over high heat. Return chicken to pan, cover, and immediately remove from heat. Let steep (do *not* uncover) for 25 minutes. Chicken is done when meat is opaque and barely pink-tinged at center. Remove chicken from liquid, cover, and refrigerate for at least 30 minutes or until next day.

Remove chicken from bones in long shreds, discarding bones. Pre- pare Tarragon-Lemon Vinaigrette. In a 2-quart bowl, lightly mix chicken with half the dressing.

Line a platter or individual plates with grape leaves. Spoon chicken mixture over leaves; arrange grapes beside or around chicken. Serve remaining dressing in a small bowl or pitcher to add to individual servings. Makes 4 servings.

Tarragon-Lemon Vinaigrette. In a small bowl, combine ¼ cup *each* **salad oil** and **lemon juice,** 1 teaspoon **dry tarragon,** ½ teaspoon **sugar,** and ¼ teaspoon *each* grated **lemon rind** and **ground cinnamon.** Whisk until thoroughly blended.

Per serving: 38 grams protein, 22 grams carbohydrates, 18 grams total fat, 11 grams unsaturated fat, 0 milligrams cholesterol, 4 milligrams sodium.

CHICKEN SALAD WITH SPICED SESAME SAUCE

Preparation time: 40 minutes
Cooking time: 25 minutes

Calories per serving: 174

3 chicken breast halves (½ lb. *each*)
1 green onion
1 slice fresh ginger (about 1 inch in diameter)
1 tablespoon dry sherry
½ teaspoon sugar
2 cups water
Spiced Sesame Sauce (recipe follows)
3 cups shredded iceberg lettuce

Creamy sesame seed tahini flavors the spicy dressing for this chicken salad; look for tahini in health food stores or stores that stock Middle Eastern foods.

In a 2-quart pan, combine chicken, onion, ginger, sherry, sugar, and water. Bring to a boil over medium-high heat; reduce heat, cover, and simmer until meat in thickest portion is no longer pink when slashed (about 20 minutes). Remove chicken from broth and let stand just until cool enough to touch. Remove chicken from bones in long shreds, discarding skin and bones. (At this point, you may cover and refrigerate until next day.)

Prepare Spiced Sesame Sauce. Mound lettuce on a platter or individual plates. Arrange chicken over lettuce. Drizzle with sesame sauce. Makes 4 servings.

Spiced Sesame Sauce. In a small bowl, combine 2 tablespoons *each* **sesame tahini** and **soy sauce** with 2 teaspoons **distilled white vinegar.** Blend in ½ teaspoon **sesame oil,** ¼ teaspoon **ground red pepper** (cayenne), 1 **green onion** (including top), sliced, and 1 tablespoon chopped **fresh cilantro** (coriander). Whisk until thoroughly blended. Mix in 1 tablespoon **water.**

If made ahead, let stand at room temperature for up to 8 hours. Stir well before serving.

Per serving: 29 grams protein, 4 grams carbohydrates, 4 grams total fat, .47 gram unsaturated fat, 0 milligrams cholesterol, 664 milligrams sodium.

Crunchy Chicken Salad Sandwiches

Seasoned yogurt dressing and crunchy water chestnuts make this chicken salad just right for light summer sandwiches.

- ⅓ cup plain yogurt
- 1 teaspoon soy sauce
- 1 teaspoon grated fresh ginger or ¼ teaspoon ground ginger
- 2 teaspoons Dijon mustard
- 1 cup skinned and shredded cooked chicken
- ½ cup slivered water chestnuts
- 2 green onions (including tops), thinly sliced
- 1 cup fresh bean sprouts
- 2 pocket breads, halved and warmed

In a medium-size bowl, combine yogurt, soy sauce, ginger, and mustard; stir until thoroughly blended. Add chicken, water chestnuts, onions, and bean sprouts; mix lightly to coat with dressing. Evenly spoon into pocket bread halves. Makes 4 sandwiches. *Calories per serving:* 166.

Biarritz Sandwiches

For a colorful and dramatic presentation, reassemble these sandwiches into a baguette shape.

- 1 can (6½ oz.) tuna packed in water, drained
- 1 hard-cooked egg, chopped
- 1 tablespoon *each* plain yogurt and Dijon mustard
- ¼ cup chopped green bell pepper
- 1 long, thin loaf French bread (12 oz.)
- 1 small avocado
- 1 medium-size tomato, sliced
- 1 cup alfalfa sprouts

In a medium-size bowl, combine tuna, egg, yogurt, mustard, and bell pepper; mix until well combined. Cut bread into 4 equal sandwich-size rolls; split each in half lengthwise.

Pit, peel, and slice avocado. Spread a fourth of the tuna mixture over each roll; add a fourth *each* of the avocado and tomato slices and ¼ cup of the sprouts. Cover with tops of rolls, fasten each with a pick, and serve immediately. Makes 4 sandwiches. *Calories per serving:* 452.

Deviled Tofu Salad Sandwiches

Tofu combines with vegetables and peanuts for a unique sandwich filling.

- 1 pound medium-firm tofu (bean curd), drained
- ½ cup *each* shredded carrot, finely chopped celery, and thinly sliced green onions (including tops)
- ⅓ cup dry roasted peanuts, chopped
- 2 tablespoons *each* lemon juice and Dijon mustard
- 1 tablespoon *each* dry basil and white wine vinegar
- 1 large clove garlic, minced or pressed
- ¼ teaspoon salt
- Dash of liquid hot pepper seasoning
- 12 slices whole-grain bread, toasted
- Lettuce leaves (optional)

Slice tofu in half. Place in a colander and let stand for 20 minutes; pat dry with paper towels. Crumble tofu into a bowl; add carrot, celery, onions, and peanuts.

In a small bowl, combine lemon juice, mustard, basil, vinegar, garlic, salt, and hot pepper seasoning; stir until thoroughly blended. Pour over tofu mixture and stir gently. Cover and refrigerate for at least 4 hours or until next day.

Spread salad evenly on 6 bread slices; top with lettuce, if desired, and cover with remaining bread slices. Makes 6 sandwiches. *Calories per serving:* 215.

SANDWICHES WITH A DIFFERENCE

If you think of a sandwich as a salad that happens to include bread, you can create delicious sandwiches that are surprisingly low in calories. When they're packed with protein as these sandwiches are, they'll be nutritionally balanced, too.

HERBED CARROTS & WILD RICE
(Pictured on page 66)

Preparation time: 30 minutes
Cooking time: About 30 minutes

Calories per serving: 129

2	**tablespoons butter or margarine**
2	**packages (12 oz. *each*) fresh baby carrots**
⅓	**cup wild rice, rinsed and drained**
⅛	**teaspoon white pepper**
1	**cup regular-strength chicken broth**
2	**tablespoons finely chopped fresh oregano leaves or 2 teaspoons dry oregano leaves; or ⅓ cup finely chopped fresh mint leaves or 2 tablespoons dry mint leaves**
2	**tablespoons lemon juice**
	Oregano, mint, or parsley sprigs

What could be a more elegant side dish for any menu than delicate baby carrots steamed on a bed of savory wild rice? The distinctive flavor comes from fresh herbs—we suggest oregano or mint, but you can try another herb of your choice.

In a wide frying pan, melt butter over medium-high heat. Add carrots, rice, pepper, and broth. Reduce heat, cover, and boil very gently until carrots and rice are tender to bite (about 30 minutes).

Add chopped oregano and lemon juice, stirring gently to blend. Transfer to a serving dish and garnish with oregano sprigs. Makes 6 servings.

Per serving: 3 grams protein, 19 grams carbohydrates, 5 grams total fat, 2 grams unsaturated fat, 14 milligrams cholesterol, 262 milligrams sodium.

ZUCCHINI BAKE

Preparation time: 25 minutes
Baking time: 35 to 40 minutes

Calories per serving: 109

4	**medium-size zucchini (about 1½ lbs. *total*)**
½	**teaspoon salt**
3	**eggs**
3	**tablespoons all-purpose flour**
¼	**cup grated Parmesan cheese**
1	**clove garlic, minced or pressed**
¾	**teaspoon oregano leaves**
⅛	**teaspoon pepper**
¼	**cup *each* finely chopped parsley and sliced green onions (including tops)**
	Vegetable oil cooking spray
15	**cherry tomatoes, halved**

When is a quiche not a quiche? When it's a no-crust egg-based casserole, bright with cherry tomatoes and low-calorie zucchini. Bake it along with a roast chicken for a light but filling meal.

Using a food processor or grater, coarsely shred zucchini (you should have about 4 cups). Sprinkle with salt; let stand in a colander for 15 minutes. Squeeze with your hands to press out moisture.

In a large bowl, beat eggs; then beat in flour, 2 tablespoons of the cheese, garlic, oregano, and pepper. Stir in parsley, onions, and zucchini.

Spray a shallow 1½-quart baking dish with cooking spray. Spread zucchini mixture in baking dish. Arrange tomato halves, cut sides up, over top, pressing in lightly. Sprinkle with remaining cheese. Bake, uncovered, in a 350° oven until egg mixture is set in center when lightly touched (35 to 40 minutes). Makes 6 servings.

Per serving: 7 grams protein, 12 grams carbohydrates, 4 grams total fat, 2 grams unsaturated fat, 130 milligrams cholesterol, 237 milligrams sodium.

MATCHSTICK ZUCCHINI
(Pictured on page 71)

(Pictured on page 71)

Preparation time: 10 minutes
Cooking time: 3 to 4 minutes

Calories per serving: 61

4	**medium-size zucchini (about 1½ lbs. *total*)**
1	**tablespoon olive oil or salad oil**
2	**cloves garlic, minced or pressed**
	Pepper
	Grated Parmesan cheese (optional)

For a pastalike side dish that's light on calories, quickly sauté thinly sliced zucchini. A tablespoon of grated Parmesan cheese on each serving adds 35 calories.

Cut zucchini into thin lengthwise slices. With a knife or a food processor fitted with a slicing disc, cut slices into long matchstick pieces.

Heat oil in a wide nonstick frying pan over medium heat. Add zucchini and garlic and cook, lifting and gently stirring, just until zucchini is tender-crisp (2 to 3 minutes). Season to taste with pepper and serve immediately. Offer cheese to sprinkle over individual servings, if desired. Makes 4 servings.

Per serving: 2 grams protein, 7 grams carbohydrates, 4 grams total fat, 3 grams unsaturated fat, 0 milligrams cholesterol, 2 milligrams sodium.

LIGHT TOUCHES: SEASONING VEGETABLES

To enhance the flavor of cooked vegetables, experiment with seasonings that don't add calories in the form of fat.

Try a squeeze of juice from a fresh lemon, lime, or orange—it can give a flavor boost to anything from asparagus to zucchini. Or mix minced garlic with freshly ground pepper for a little zip. Snipped fresh or crushed dried herbs contribute a fascinating array of tastes; use them singly or in combination. Thinly sliced green onions or finely chopped parsley or cilantro add flavor as well as color and make wonderful garnishes, too.

VEGETABLES WITH LEMON-DILL DRESSING

Preparation time: 25 minutes

Calories per serving: 74

2	**cups bite-size cauliflower flowerets**
3	**medium-size carrots (about ½ lb. *total*), thinly sliced**
¼	**pound mushrooms, thinly sliced**
	Lemon-Dill Dressing (recipe follows)
	Chopped parsley

Toss cauliflower, carrots, and mushrooms in a zesty lemon-dill dressing for a colorful side dish that contains both vitamin C and iron.

Combine cauliflower, carrots, and mushrooms in a large bowl. Prepare Lemon-Dill Dressing and add to vegetables, mixing lightly. Sprinkle with parsley. If made ahead, cover and let stand for up to 30 minutes. Makes 6 servings.

Lemon-Dill Dressing. In a small bowl, combine 2 tablespoons **salad oil;** ¼ cup **lemon juice;** 1 clove **garlic,** minced or pressed; ¼ teaspoon *each* **salt, dry mustard, dill weed,** and grated **lemon peel;** and ⅛ teaspoon **pepper.** Whisk until thoroughly blended.

Per serving: 2 grams protein, 7 grams carbohydrates, 5 grams total fat, 4 grams unsaturated fat, 0 milligrams cholesterol, 114 milligrams sodium.

ROASTED NEW POTATOES

Preparation time: 10 minutes
Baking time: 40 to 45 minutes

Calories per serving: 88

2 tablespoons butter or margarine, melted

¼ teaspoon *each* marjoram leaves and salt

⅛ teaspoon pepper

1 pound small new red potatoes (1½ to 2 inches in diameter), well scrubbed

2 small onions, cut lengthwise into quarters

Lemon wedges

Tempting aromas announce something special's in the oven when you roast tiny new potatoes and onion wedges along with chicken. When everything's ready, squeeze on a bit of fresh lemon juice.

Combine butter, marjoram, salt, and pepper in a shallow 1½- to 2-quart baking dish. Add potatoes and onions, turning to coat with butter mixture. Cover and bake in a 400° oven until potatoes are tender when pierced (40 to 45 minutes). Serve with lemon wedges. Makes 6 servings.

Per serving: 2 grams protein, 12 grams carbohydrates, 4 grams total fat, 1 gram unsaturated fat, 12 milligrams cholesterol, 51 milligrams sodium.

VEGETABLE & BULGUR STIR-FRY

Preparation time: 20 minutes
Cooking time: About 20 minutes

Calories per serving: 285

2 medium-size carrots

1 medium-size zucchini

1 medium-size crookneck squash

¼ pound mushrooms

2 tablespoons salad oil

1 cup bulgur

1 tablespoon sesame seeds

1 clove garlic, minced or pressed

1½ teaspoons Italian herb seasoning or ½ teaspoon *each* dry basil, marjoram leaves, and oregano leaves

⅛ teaspoon pepper

1¾ cups water

2 cups broccoli flowerets

½ cup shredded jack cheese

½ cup sliced green onions (including tops)

3 pocket breads, halved and warmed (optional)

Lemon wedges

Here's a versatile vegetable dish, bright as a garden with half a dozen different vegetables. You can serve it as a side dish—with grilled chicken or fish—for six or as a vegetarian main dish for four. The stir-fry can also be spooned into warm pita bread halves (add 75 calories for each) to make a satisfying sandwich.

Thinly slice carrots, zucchini, crookneck squash, and mushrooms; set aside in separate piles.

Heat 1 tablespoon of the oil in a wide nonstick frying pan over medium-high heat. Add bulgur, sesame seeds, and carrots; stir-fry for 2 minutes. Add remaining 1 tablespoon oil, garlic, zucchini, crookneck squash, and mushrooms; stir-fry for 2 more minutes. Add herb seasoning, pepper, and water; reduce heat, cover, and simmer until liquid is absorbed (about 10 minutes).

Add broccoli; cover and cook for 2 minutes. Stir in cheese. Sprinkle with onions and spoon into pocket bread halves, if desired. Serve with lemon wedges. Makes 6 servings.

Per serving: 11 grams protein, 42 grams carbohydrates, 9 grams total fat, 5 grams unsaturated fat, 9 milligrams cholesterol, 95 milligrams sodium.

IN THE
SPOTLIGHT:
VEGETARIAN
MAIN DISHES

To find a low-calorie, low-cholesterol meal that's delicious and a little bit different, look no further. These vegetarian dishes, appealing alternatives to meat, poultry, and seafood, feature combinations of ingredients that provide the complete protein you need for your main meal. They also offer exciting adventures in flavor.

Asian-style Pasta Primavera

East meets West when Oriental vegetables and asparagus are tossed with linguine in this light and unusual pasta creation. If you can't find bok choy, you can substitute Swiss chard.

  3 tablespoons sesame seeds
  8 large dry or fresh shiitake mushrooms (about 3 inches in diameter) or ½ pound fresh mushrooms
  ½ pound *each* asparagus and bok choy
  6 ounces linguine
  2 tablespoons salad oil
  2 cloves garlic, minced or pressed
  1 tablespoon very finely chopped fresh ginger
  ½ pound Chinese pea pods (snow or sugar peas), ends and strings removed
  ¼ cup dry sherry
  1 cup regular-strength chicken broth
  2 tablespoons soy sauce
  1 teaspoon *each* sugar and white wine vinegar

In a wok or wide frying pan, toast sesame seeds over medium-low heat, shaking pan often, until golden (2 to 3 minutes). Pour out seeds and set aside.

If using dry mushrooms, soak in hot water until soft (about 20 minutes) drain well. Cut off and discard tough stems of dry or fresh shiitake mushrooms; thinly slice mushrooms.

Snap off and discard tough ends of asparagus; cut asparagus spears and bok choy stems and leaves into ½-inch diagonal slices. Set vegetables aside.

In a 4- to 5-quart pan, cook linguine in 3 to 4 quarts of boiling water just until barely tender to bite (8 to 10 minutes); drain well. Place in a large shallow serving bowl and keep warm.

Add oil to wok or frying pan and place over high heat. Add garlic and ginger; cook, stirring constantly, until lightly browned (about 30 seconds). Add mushrooms, asparagus, bok choy, pea pods, and sherry. Cover and cook, stirring once or twice, until vegetables are bright green and tender-crisp (about 2 minutes). Spoon over noodles.

To same pan add broth, soy sauce, sugar, and vinegar; bring to a boil, stirring. Pour over noodles and vegetables. Sprinkle with sesame seeds, then mix lightly. Serve immediately. Makes 4 servings. *Calories per serving:* 355.

Baked Spinach Crêpes

Fresh spinach in the batter and parsley-flecked ricotta cheese in the filling make these crêpes a light and nutritious main-dish choice. Top them with a quick and easy tomato sauce for added color and zest.

  ½ pound spinach
  3 eggs
  1 tablespoon salad oil
  1 cup all-purpose flour
  1½ cups nonfat milk
    Herbed Tomato Sauce (recipe follows)
    Vegetable oil cooking spray
  1 cup part-skim milk ricotta cheese
  ¼ cup chopped parsley
  2 tablespoons grated Parmesan cheese

Remove and discard tough stems from spinach. Rinse leaves well and coarsely chop. In a blender or food processor, combine spinach, eggs, and oil; whirl until smooth. Add flour and whirl again; add milk and whirl, stopping motor once or twice to scrape sides of container, until no lumps of flour remain. Cover batter and refrigerate.

Meanwhile, prepare Herbed Tomato Sauce; while it cooks, make crêpes.

Spray a 6- to 7-inch crêpe pan with cooking spray; heat pan over medium heat until a drop of water dances on surface. Pour about 3 tablespoons of the batter into pan, tilting pan so batter covers entire surface. Cook until top is dry and edges are lightly browned. Carefully turn and brown other side. Turn out onto a plate. Repeat, stacking crêpes as they're made. Use more cooking spray as needed if crêpes begin to stick.

In a bowl, mix ricotta cheese and parsley. Spread half the tomato sauce in a shallow 3-quart baking dish. Using about 1 tablespoon of the cheese mixture for each, spread cheese filling in a strip at one side of each crêpe; roll up and place, side by side, in baking dish. Spoon remaining tomato sauce over crêpes. Sprinkle with Parmesan cheese. (At this point, you may cover and refrigerate until next day.)

Bake, uncovered, in a 350° oven until heated through (about 20 minutes or, if refrigerated, up to 35 minutes). Makes 6 servings. *Calories per serving: 280.*

Herbed Tomato Sauce. Heat 1 tablespoon **olive oil** in a wide nonstick frying pan over medium heat; add 1 small **onion,** finely chopped; ¼ pound **mushrooms,** thinly sliced; and 1 teaspoon **herbes de Provence** or ¼ teaspoon *each* dry basil and marjoram, oregano, and thyme leaves. Cook, stirring often, until onion is soft (about 5 minutes).

Stir in 1 clove **garlic,** minced or pressed, and 1 can (about 1 lb.) ready-cut **tomatoes.** Bring to a boil and cook, uncovered, stirring often, until sauce is thickened and reduced to about 2 cups (about 10 minutes).

Vegetable Burgers with Peanut Sauce

Zippy peanut sauce lends a taste of Southeast Asia—as well as protein—to these vegetable patties.

> Peanut Sauce (recipe follows)
> 1 **tablespoon sesame seeds**
> 2 **eggs**
> 2 **teaspoons soy sauce**
> ½ **teaspoon ground pepper**
> 5 **slices day-old whole-grain bread, finely diced (about 3 cups** *total***)**
> 1 **large onion, finely chopped**
> 1 **large red or green bell pepper, seeded and finely chopped**
> 1 **stalk celery, finely chopped**
> ½ **cup** *each* **shredded carrot and zucchini**
> 1 **tablespoon butter or margarine**

Prepare Peanut Sauce.

Toast sesame seeds in a small frying pan over medium-low heat, shaking pan often, until golden (2 to 3 minutes).

Break eggs into a large bowl. Add sesame seeds, soy sauce, and ground pepper; beat until well combined. Stir in bread, onion, bell pepper, celery, carrot, and zucchini. Divide mixture into 8 equal balls, then flatten each into a patty about ¾ inch thick.

In a wide nonstick frying pan, melt butter over medium-high heat. Add patties and cook, carefully turning once, until browned on both sides (about 8 minutes *total*). Serve warm with sauce. Makes 4 servings, 2 patties each. *Calories per serving: 301.*

Peanut Sauce. In a small bowl, combine 2 tablespoons *each* **creamy peanut butter** and **soy sauce;** 1 tablespoon *each* **sugar, salad oil,** and **distilled white vinegar;** 1 teaspoon **sesame oil;** 2 **green onions** (including tops), minced; and ¼ to ½ teaspoon **ground red pepper** (cayenne). Mix until well combined. Makes about ½ cup.

E·G·G·S &

Eggs and cheese deliver vitamins and minerals, complete protein, and fresh flavor all in one package. These nutritious, versatile foods can play starring or supporting roles at almost any meal with equal ease. In fact, much of the world's finest cuisine—as well as plenty of hearty, more humble fare—is based on eggs and cheese.

But even though these foods are delicious and rich in many essential nutrients, good sense counsels eating them in moderation. The yolk of an egg is a concentrated source of cholesterol (it contains an entire day's quota), and a number of respected nutritionists recommend limiting egg yolks to three or four a week. Many cheeses, as well, are high in both fat and cholesterol.

For this reason, our recipes take the light approach to these foods, carefully controlling the amounts in each serving without sacrificing good flavor.

Cooking with Cheese

Cheese varies widely in both flavor and texture, as anyone who has ever shopped for cheese knows. It can be mild or sharp, creamy or crumbly. A soft, mild variety like ricotta can enhance a sweet dish, such as our luscious Ricotta Pancakes (facing page); a tangy variety like goat cheese can add zing to a savory entrée. Sometimes, just a sprinkling of a distinctive cheese like Swiss or blue cheese can wake up a plain omelet.

In our light approach to cooking with cheese, we use high-fat cheeses sparingly, adding just a small amount for a flavorful finishing touch. Our Artichoke-Olive Soufflé (page 46)

For versatility, nutrition, and just plain good flavor, eggs and cheese are hard to beat. You can serve them at any meal, anytime, in a hundred different ways. Try our fresh, light approach and you'll create dishes that are new, exciting, *and* low in calories!

uses just an ounce of shredded Swiss cheese per serving, deriving much of its delicious flavor from artichokes and olives rather than from a large amount of cheese.

When possible, we call for lowfat cheeses in our recipes. The filling of Mushroom-crust Quiche (page 45) relies on lowfat cottage cheese, a little Swiss cheese, and eggs. For information on selecting cheeses that are lower in fat (and calories), see page 44.

Cooking with Eggs

Eggs are the perfect food for breakfast, brunch, lunch, or supper—and for virtually any occasion. You can make them the center of attraction —scrambled, poached, baked, or whipped into an omelet—or use them as the base for main dishes such as frittatas, soufflés, and quiches. In this chapter, you'll find recipes for all these options and more.

When it comes to cooking with eggs, we show you a few tricks for doing it the light way. Generally, our recipes call for fewer eggs per serving than do more traditional dishes, but you'd never know it. What's the secret? We replace a few of the high-fat whole eggs in a recipe with egg whites (which contain protein but only the slightest trace of fat).

Another light cooking method is to extend a small amount of egg with lowfat milk or with appetizing fresh vegetables and fruits. In Zucchini Omelets (page 44), there's only one egg per omelet, yet the tender-crisp shredded zucchini in each omelet stretches one egg into a satisfying serving that's low in fat and calories.

C·H·E·E·S·E

CINNAMON-APPLE DUTCH BABY
(Pictured on page 42)

Preparation time: 20 minutes
Baking time: 15 to 20 minutes

Calories per serving: 196

2 tablespoons butter or margarine

2 teaspoons ground cinnamon

3 tablespoons granulated sugar

2 medium-size tart cooking apples, such as Gravenstein or Granny Smith, peeled and cored

Vegetable oil cooking spray

3 eggs

¾ cup *each* lowfat milk and all-purpose flour

Powdered sugar

Fragrant with cinnamon, this oven pancake makes weekend breakfast a real treat! The secrets of its lightness? Lowfat milk and a reduced amount of butter.

In a shallow 2- to 3-quart baking pan (such as a round or oval au gratin pan or a frying pan with an ovenproof handle), melt butter over medium heat; stir in cinnamon and granulated sugar. Thinly slice apples into pan. Cook, stirring, until apples begin to soften (about 5 minutes). Spray inside edge of pan with cooking spray. Place pan, uncovered, in a 425° oven for 5 minutes.

Meanwhile, break eggs into a blender or food processor and whirl at high speed for 1 minute. With motor running, gradually pour in milk, then slowly add flour; continue whirling for 30 seconds. (Or, in a bowl, beat eggs until blended; gradually beat in milk, then flour.)

Remove pan from oven and pour in batter. Return to oven and bake until pancake is puffy and well browned (15 to 20 minutes). Dust with powdered sugar, cut into wedges, and serve immediately. Makes 6 servings.

Per serving: 6 grams protein, 26 grams carbohydrates, 8 grams total fat, 3 grams unsaturated fat, 141 milligrams cholesterol, 97 milligrams sodium.

RICOTTA PANCAKES

Preparation time: 15 minutes
Cooking time: 20 minutes

Calories per serving: 157

3 eggs, separated

1 cup part-skim-milk ricotta cheese

⅓ cup lowfat milk

½ cup all-purpose flour

2 teaspoons sugar

½ teaspoon baking powder

¼ teaspoon salt

Vegetable oil cooking spray

2 peaches, peeled and thinly sliced

Warm honey (optional)

Juicy peach slices make a refreshing topping for these light, moist pancakes, made with ricotta cheese. A drizzle of warm honey will add about 60 calories per tablespoon.

In a food processor or blender, combine egg yolks and ricotta. Whirl until blended. Add milk, flour, sugar, baking powder, and salt; whirl until mixture is well combined. In a large bowl, beat egg whites until stiff, moist peaks form; gently fold in batter.

Preheat a griddle or wide frying pan over medium heat; spray with cooking spray. Using about ¼ cup for each pancake, pour batter onto hot griddle. Cook until tops of pancakes are bubbly and appear dry; turn and cook other sides until browned.

Top pancakes with peach slices; drizzle with honey, if desired. Makes about 1 dozen 4-inch pancakes (6 servings).

Per serving: 9 grams protein, 16 grams carbohydrates, 6 grams total fat, 2 grams unsaturated fat, 139 milligrams cholesterol, 175 milligrams sodium.

Welcome Sunday morning at your house with
the cozy-warm aroma of cinnamon and apples when you bake
a light, puffy Cinnamon-Apple Dutch Baby (page 41). Lowfat milk and reduced
amounts of butter make our version feather-light.

OMELET WITH JULIENNE VEGETABLES

Preparation time: 30 minutes
Cooking time: 12 to 15 minutes

Calories per serving: 341

4	large dried Oriental or fresh mushrooms
	Sherry-Soy Sauce (recipe follows)
1	tablespoon salad oil
1	medium-size carrot, cut into julienne strips
1	stalk celery, cut into julienne strips
4	eggs
2	tablespoons water
	Vegetable oil cooking spray
1	tablespoon butter or margarine

A simple omelet becomes a special supper for two when you top it with this distinctive sherry-flavored vegetable sauce.

Soak dried mushrooms in hot water to cover until soft (about 30 minutes); drain well. Discard stems and cut into thin strips (or sliver fresh mushrooms, including stems).

Prepare Sherry-Soy Sauce; set aside. Heat oil in a medium-size non-stick frying pan over medium heat. Add carrot, celery, and mushrooms; cook, stirring often, until carrot is tender-crisp (4 to 5 minutes). Add sauce and cook, stirring, until sauce thickens and boils. Remove from heat and keep warm.

In a large bowl, beat eggs and water until well blended. Spray a 10-inch nonstick omelet pan with cooking spray; add butter and place over medium-high heat until butter is melted. Tilt pan to coat bottom and sides with butter. Pour in egg mixture and cook, gently lifting cooked portion to let uncooked egg flow underneath. Shake pan often to keep omelet from sticking.

Continue cooking until eggs are set but top still looks moist. Remove from heat. Fold a third of the omelet over center; slide unfolded edge onto a warm serving plate. Then flip folded portion over on top. Spoon vegetable sauce over omelet. Makes 2 servings.

Sherry-Soy Sauce. In a small bowl, combine 1 teaspoon *each* **cornstarch** and **sugar,** 1 tablespoon **dry sherry,** 2 tablespoons **soy sauce,** and ¼ cup **water;** stir until well blended.

Per serving: 15 grams protein, 13 grams carbohydrates, 25 grams total fat, 13 grams unsaturated fat, 524 milligrams cholesterol, 1557 milligrams sodium.

CHEESE & BASIL OMELET

Preparation time: 5 minutes
Cooking time: 8 to 10 minutes

Calories per serving: 223

1½ to 2	ounces goat cheese or blue cheese
6	eggs
2	egg whites
3	tablespoons water
¼	teaspoon salt
⅛	teaspoon white pepper
2	tablespoons butter or margarine
1	clove garlic, minced or pressed
3	tablespoons lightly packed chopped fresh basil leaves

Serve this generous basil- and goat cheese-filled omelet along with sliced tomatoes for a summer supper. Combining whole eggs and egg whites lowers the calorie and cholesterol totals.

Cut off and discard any rind from goat cheese. Coarsely crumble cheese and set aside. In a large bowl, combine eggs, egg whites, water, salt, and pepper; beat with a wire whisk or fork until well combined.

In a 10-inch nonstick omelet or frying pan, melt butter over medium heat; add garlic, tilting pan to coat bottom and sides with butter mixture. Pour in egg mixture and cook, gently lifting cooked portion to let uncooked egg flow underneath. Shake pan often to keep omelet from sticking.

When eggs are about half set, sprinkle with basil and cheese. Continue cooking until eggs are set but top still looks moist. Holding pan over a warm serving plate, shake so half of omelet slides out onto plate; then quickly flick pan over so omelet folds onto itself on plate. Makes 4 servings.

Per serving: 14 grams protein, 1 gram carbohydrates, 18 grams total fat, 8 grams unsaturated fat, 407 milligrams cholesterol, 394 milligrams sodium.

ZUCCHINI OMELETS

Preparation time: 15 minutes
Cooking time: 12 to 15 minutes

Calories per serving: 158

3 small zucchini (about ½ lb. *total*)

4 eggs

¼ teaspoon *each* ground nutmeg, pepper, and salt

1½ tablespoons finely chopped parsley

4 teaspoons butter or margarine

¼ cup shredded Swiss cheese

Top these fresh-tasting omelets with cold Fresh Tomato Salsa (page 92) or hot Herbed Tomato Sauce (page 39) for extra pizzazz.

Using a food processor or grater, finely shred zucchini. Squeeze with your hands to press out moisture (you should have about 1 cup). In a large bowl, beat eggs, then beat in nutmeg, pepper, and salt. Stir in parsley and zucchini.

Set an 8- to 9-inch nonstick omelet pan over medium heat. For each omelet, swirl 1 teaspoon of the butter in pan until melted. Add a fourth of the egg mixture, spreading it over pan bottom with a spatula. Cook until bottom of omelet is lightly browned and top is still moist.

Remove from heat. Fold a third of the omelet over center; slide unfolded edge onto a plate. Then flip folded portion over on top. Keep warm. Cook remaining omelets in same manner. Sprinkle each omelet with 1 tablespoon of the cheese. Makes 4 servings.

Per serving: 10 grams protein, 3 grams carbohydrates, 12 grams total fat, 5 grams unsaturated fat, 274 milligrams cholesterol, 346 milligrams sodium.

LIGHT TOUCHES: CHOOSING CHEESES WISELY

Flavorful, versatile cheeses are perennial favorites for snacking, for salads and sandwiches, and for cooking. But because many cheeses are high in fat, it pays to know the score—in calories—when you choose a cheese.

Whole-milk cheeses are higher in fat than those made with part-skim or lowfat milk. When you shop for cheese, be sure to read the labels carefully so you can select the ones that are lighter.

Calories per ounce:

24	Cottage cheese (lowfat)
30	Cottage cheese (creamed)
44	Ricotta (part-skim milk)
80	Neufchâtel cream cheese
85	Mozzarella (part-skim milk)
103	Monterey jack
104	Swiss
105	Cream cheese
112	Cheddar

GREEK SCRAMBLED EGGS

Preparation time: 15 minutes
Cooking time: 10 minutes

Calories per serving: 215

8 eggs

2 egg whites

2 tablespoons water

¾ teaspoon oregano leaves

⅛ teaspoon pepper

2 tablespoons butter or margarine

½ cup crumbled feta cheese

1 medium-size tomato

¼ cup chopped parsley

10 to 12 whole Greek olives or ripe olives

A spirited topping of feta cheese, olives, parsley, and chopped tomato lends a Mediterranean touch to these light and fluffy scrambled eggs.

In a large bowl, combine eggs, egg whites, water , oregano, and pepper; beat with a wire whisk or fork until well blended. In a wide ovenproof nonstick frying pan, melt butter over low heat. Pour in egg mixture; as it sets, push cooked egg aside with a wide spatula so uncooked portion can flow underneath. Continue cooking just until eggs are softly set.

Sprinkle cheese evenly over eggs. Place pan under a broiler about 4 inches below heat and broil just until cheese is hot (1 to 2 minutes). Meanwhile, dice tomato. Sprinkle tomato and parsley evenly over eggs; garnish with olives. Serve immediately. Makes 6 servings.

Per serving: 13 grams protein, 3 grams carbohydrates, 17 grams total fat, 7 grams unsaturated fat, 366 milligrams cholesterol, 452 milligrams sodium.

ASPARAGUS & EGG RAMEKINS

Preparation time: 10 minutes
Baking time: 3 minutes

Calories per serving: 232

12 spears fresh asparagus (about ½ lb. *total*)

Vegetable oil cooking spray

4 teaspoons butter or margarine

8 eggs

¼ cup grated Parmesan cheese

Coarsely ground pepper

When spring brings fresh asparagus to market, celebrate with our easy main-dish version of the Italian favorite Asparagus Milanese, made light with eggs baked in ramekins instead of fried.

Snap off and discard tough ends of asparagus; peel stalks, if desired. Arrange spears parallel in a small amount of boiling water in a wide frying pan (or place in a steamer over boiling water). Cover and boil gently (or steam) just until spears are easily pierced with a knife tip (5 to 7 minutes). Drain immediately and keep warm.

While asparagus is cooking, spray each of 4 long, shallow ramekins with cooking spray; add 1 teaspoon of the butter to each. Place ramekins on a rimmed baking sheet and heat in a 450° oven just until butter is melted (about 1 minute).

Remove ramekins from oven and carefully break 2 eggs into each. Return to oven and bake just until egg whites are set (about 2 minutes). Arrange 3 asparagus spears beside eggs in each ramekin; sprinkle each with 1 tablespoon of the cheese. Return to oven and bake for 1 more minute. Serve immediately. Season to taste with pepper. Makes 4 servings.

Per serving: 16 grams protein, 4 grams carbohydrates, 17 grams total fat, 8 grams unsaturated fat, 523 milligrams cholesterol, 207 milligrams sodium.

MUSHROOM-CRUST QUICHE

Preparation time: 30 minutes
Baking time: 25 to 30 minutes

Calories per serving: 223

Vegetable oil cooking spray

3 tablespoons butter or margarine

½ pound mushrooms, finely chopped

½ cup finely crushed saltine crackers

¾ cup thinly sliced green onions (including tops)

1 cup (4 oz.) shredded Swiss cheese

1 cup lowfat cottage cheese

3 eggs

¼ teaspoon ground red pepper (cayenne)

⅛ teaspoon paprika

Chopped sautéed mushrooms, lightly bound with cracker crumbs, make the low-calorie crust for this rich-tasting quiche.

Spray bottom and sides of a 9-inch pie pan with cooking spray. In a medium-size nonstick frying pan, melt 2 tablespoons of the butter over medium heat. Add mushrooms and cook, stirring often, until most of the moisture has evaporated and mushrooms are lightly browned. Stir in crushed crackers, then turn mixture into prepared pie pan. Press evenly over bottom and sides of pan.

In same frying pan, melt remaining 1 tablespoon butter over medium heat; add onions and cook, stirring, just until soft and bright green. Spoon onions evenly over crust and sprinkle with Swiss cheese. In a blender or food processor, combine cottage cheese, eggs, and red pepper; whirl until smooth. Pour into crust; sprinkle with paprika.

Bake in a 350° oven until a knife inserted just off center comes out clean (25 to 30 minutes). Let stand for about 5 minutes before cutting into wedges. Makes 6 servings.

Per serving: 14 grams protein, 8 grams carbohydrates, 15 grams total fat, 6 grams unsaturated fat, 165 milligrams cholesterol, 375 milligrams sodium.

ARTICHOKE-OLIVE SOUFFLÉ
(Pictured on facing page)

Preparation time: 30 minutes
Baking time: 30 to 35 minutes

Calories per serving: 392

3	tablespoons butter or margarine
3	tablespoons all-purpose flour
½	teaspoon salt
¾	cup nonfat milk
1	cup (4 oz.) shredded Swiss cheese
1	jar (6 oz.) marinated artichoke hearts, drained and coarsely chopped
1	small can (2¼ oz.) sliced ripe olives, well drained
5	eggs, separated
	Vegetable oil cooking spray
1	tablespoon grated Parmesan cheese

Here's a spectacular brunch or vegetarian supper entrée that really is as light as it looks. Made with nonfat milk and a moderate amount of cheese, it gets its provocative flavor from marinated artichokes and ripe olives.

In a 2-quart pan, melt butter over medium heat. Add flour and salt and cook, stirring, until bubbly. Remove from heat and gradually blend in milk until smooth. Return to heat and cook, stirring constantly, until mixture boils and thickens. Add Swiss cheese and stir until cheese is melted. Blend in artichokes and olives. Remove from heat. With a wooden spoon, beat in egg yolks.

Spray bottom and sides of a 1½- to 2-quart soufflé dish with cooking spray, then coat with Parmesan cheese. In a bowl, whip egg whites until moist, soft peaks form. Gently fold egg whites into cheese sauce. Pour mixture into prepared baking dish. Bake in a 375° oven until soufflé is puffy and golden brown and a long pick inserted in center (through a surface crack) comes out clean (30 to 35 minutes). Serve immediately. Makes 4 servings.

Per serving: 19 grams protein, 10 grams carbohydrates, 26 grams total fat, 11 grams unsaturated fat, 373 milligrams cholesterol, 773 milligrams sodium.

BAKED BROCCOLI FRITTATA

Preparation time: 25 minutes
Baking time: 25 to 30 minutes

Calories per serving: 164

1	tablespoon olive oil
1	tablespoon butter or margarine
1	medium-size onion, finely chopped
1	clove garlic, minced or pressed
¼	cup chopped parsley
2	cups finely chopped broccoli (flowerets and top portion of stems)
½	teaspoon dry basil
¼	cup grated Parmesan cheese
¼	teaspoon salt
⅛	teaspoon pepper
6	eggs
2	egg whites
	Vegetable oil cooking spray
	Lemon wedges

Bake this light, broccoli-studded egg dish to golden perfection in the oven, then serve it hot or at room temperature anytime—for lunch, brunch, supper, or even on a picnic.

Heat oil and butter in a wide non-stick frying pan over medium heat; add onion and cook, stirring often, until onion begins to soften (about 3 minutes). Stir in garlic, parsley, broccoli, and basil; continue cooking, stirring often, until broccoli is bright green (about 3 minutes). Remove from heat and stir in 2 tablespoons of the cheese, salt, and pepper.

In a large bowl, beat eggs and egg whites until well blended; stir in broccoli mixture. Spray a shallow 2-quart baking dish with cooking spray. Pour in broccoli mixture; sprinkle evenly with remaining cheese. Bake, uncovered, in a 350° oven until frittata is firm in center when touched (25 to 30 minutes). Serve warm or at room temperature; accompany with lemon wedges. Makes 6 servings.

Per serving: 11 grams protein, 6 grams carbohydrates, 11 grams total fat, 6 grams unsaturated fat, 262 milligrams cholesterol, 223 milligrams sodium.

The lively flavors of ripe olives and
marinated artichokes lend pizzazz to light-as-a-cloud
Artichoke-Olive Soufflé (facing page). Nonfat milk and a moderate amount
of cheese ensure a low calorie count.

F·I·S·H &

It's no surprise that as interest in light, healthy eating has grown, fish and shellfish have finally come into their own. Today, fresh fish and shellfish are turning up in all the best places—in stylish restaurants, in well-stocked supermarkets, and on the table in homes where healthy eating is the order of the day. And they're being prepared in fresh new ways that enhance their delicate flavors and natural lightness.

As you'll see in this chapter, there's much more to preparing fish than frying it in fat or broiling it to an unappetizing dryness. Instead, we marinate it, wrap it elegantly in parchment paper, stuff it with a mélange of fresh vegetables, even toss it with pasta. The results are light, moist, and never dull!

What makes fish so good for you? Fish and shellfish are top-notch sources of protein. Generally, they're also low in saturated fats (compared with other protein foods); many varieties, such as flounder, are also high in unsaturated fats, which may have a role in lowering blood cholesterol.

Because most fish and shellfish are naturally low in calories, you can serve more generous portions than with even the leanest meats. For a guide to the fat content and calories of many types of fish, see page 53.

A variety of fresh fish. Not so long ago, it was hard to find fresh fish that compared in quality and variety to that served in restaurants. But all that has changed. Tiny bay scallops, at one time a regional delicacy, are now more widely available. Bandiera Italiana (page 60) celebrates their sweet flavor and tender texture

Once served up breaded and fried, fish and shellfish are finally getting the imaginative culinary treatment they so richly deserve. With fresh, naturally light seafood and our selection of recipes, you can make dishes so good they'll be the star attraction every time!

in an unusual pasta-vegetable combination.

Monkfish, previously known only to travelers abroad, is now appearing in our fish markets. In Sautéed Monkfish with Caper Sauce (page 51), it's enlivened with a simple mustardy sauce.

And don't forget the old standbys, such as salmon and trout. Salmon with Vegetable Crest (facing page) crowns salmon steaks with a creamy topping of cheese and vegetables. And what could be more tasty than Calico Stuffed Trout (page 52), tender whole trout bursting with a vegetable-herb stuffing.

Cooking it light. No matter which cooking method you prefer, our recipes show you how to do it lightly and healthfully.

• *Grilling* and *broiling* produce juicy, delicious dishes without adding rich buttery sauces. A good example is our Grilled Tuna with Teriyaki Fruit Sauce (page 51), which pairs the fish with a light sauce and fresh fruit.

• *Baking* a panful of fish briefly in a superhot oven, as we do for Crusty Fish with Yogurt-Dill Sauce (page 59), toasts the fish golden brown on the outside, while leaving the inside moist and tender.

• *Stir-frying* or *sautéing* fish or shellfish needn't require lots of butter or oil. Stir-fried Shrimp with Peking Sauce (page 62) calls for just a touch of oil.

• *Steaming* and *poaching* produce gloriously moist fish and shellfish with no fat. And if you have a microwave oven, by all means try our *microwaving* recipes on page 56.

S·H·E·L·L·F·I·S·H

SALMON WITH VEGETABLE CREST

(Pictured on page 6)

Vegetable oil cooking spray

2 salmon or halibut steaks or fillets (about 6 oz. *each*)

3 tablespoons lemon juice

2 ounces Neufchâtel cheese, softened

⅛ teaspoon *each* salt and pepper

¼ cup *each* finely grated carrot and chopped, seeded tomato

2 tablespoons thinly sliced green onions (including tops)

1 tablespoon finely chopped parsley

Lemon or lime wedges

Preparation time: 25 minutes
Baking time: 12 to 15 minutes

Calories per serving: 428

Luscious baked salmon steaks or fillets are topped with a mixture of fluffy Neufchâtel cheese and chopped fresh vegetables in this elegant main dish. If you substitute halibut for the salmon, the dish will be about 25 percent lower in calories.

Spray a shallow baking pan with cooking spray. Place fish in a single layer in pan and drizzle with 2 tablespoons of the lemon juice. Set aside.

In a small bowl, mix cheese, salt, pepper, and remaining 1 tablespoon lemon juice until smooth and fluffy; lightly stir in carrot, tomato, onions, and parsley. Mound vegetable mixture evenly over fish, spreading nearly to edges.

Bake, uncovered, in a 400° oven until fish flakes easily when prodded in thickest portion with a fork (12 to 15 minutes). Serve with lemon wedges. Makes 2 servings.

Per serving: 36 grams protein, 7 grams carbohydrates, 18 grams total fat, 10 grams unsaturated fat, 21 milligrams cholesterol, 330 milligrams sodium.

BROILED BABY SALMON WITH SHERRY-SOY BUTTER

1 tablespoon sesame seeds

2 tablespoons butter or margarine

2 tablespoons thinly sliced green onions (including tops)

2 tablespoons dry sherry

1 tablespoon soy sauce

Vegetable oil cooking spray

4 boned baby salmon or trout (about 8 oz. *each*), heads removed

Preparation time: 10 minutes
Broiling time: 6 to 8 minutes

Calories per serving: 303

Mild-tasting baby silver salmon come to market boned and butterflied. Just brush on the flavored butter, then slip them under the broiler.

In a small frying pan, toast sesame seeds over medium-low heat, shaking pan often, until golden (2 to 3 minutes). Add butter, onions, sherry, and soy sauce; cook, stirring, until butter is melted and mixture is well combined. Remove from heat.

Spray rack of a 13- by 15-inch (or larger) broiler pan with cooking spray. Spread salmon open and place, skin side down, on rack. Brush evenly with sesame seed mixture. Broil about 4 inches below heat until fish is opaque in thickest portion when tested with a knife (6 to 8 minutes). Makes 4 servings.

Per serving: 44 grams protein, 2 grams carbohydrates, 22 grams total fat, 16 grams unsaturated fat, 125 milligrams cholesterol, 401 milligrams sodium.

The tropical flavors of Hawaii suffuse succulent
Grilled Tuna with Teriyaki Fruit Sauce (facing page). Sliced
papaya, candied ginger, and a light sherry-soy sauce top thick tuna steak;
fresh bell peppers provide a colorful garnish.

GRILLED TUNA WITH TERIYAKI FRUIT SAUCE
(Pictured on facing page)

Preparation time: 15 to 20 minutes
Grilling time: 3 to 4 minutes

Calories per serving: 267

¼ cup *each* soy sauce and sugar

6 tablespoons sake or dry sherry

3 thin slices fresh ginger or ¼ teaspoon ground ginger

1 pound boned, skinned tuna fillets or steaks (¾ to 1 inch thick), cut into 4 equal pieces

 Vegetable oil cooking spray

8 to 12 thin slices peeled, seeded papaya

2 teaspoons finely chopped candied or crystallized ginger

1 medium-size green bell pepper, seeded and cut into long, thin slivers

Experience a taste of the tropics when you grill thick fillets of fresh tuna, top them with an exotic gingered sauce, and serve with papaya, candied ginger, and green bell pepper. Tuna is substantial and satisfying, yet relatively low in fat; to keep it moist and succulent, grill it very briefly—it should be opaque on the outside but still rare in the center.

In a 2-quart pan, combine soy sauce, sugar, sake, and ginger slices; bring to a boil over high heat, stirring until sugar is dissolved. Continue boiling until reduced to ⅓ cup; discard ginger slices. Keep sauce warm.

Spray fish lightly on both sides with cooking spray. Place on a barbecue grill about 6 inches above a solid bed of hot coals. Grill, turning once, until outside is firm and opaque but inside is still translucent and moist-looking when tested with a knife (1½ to 2 minutes on each side).

Place each piece of tuna on a warm dinner plate. Top each serving with a fourth *each* of the soy sauce mixture, papaya slices, and candied ginger; arrange bell pepper pieces alongside. Makes 4 servings.

Per serving: 30 grams protein, 28 grams carbohydrates, 7 grams total fat, 6 grams unsaturated fat, 43 milligrams cholesterol, 1337 milligrams sodium.

SAUTÉED MONKFISH WITH CAPER SAUCE

Preparation time: 15 minutes
Cooking time: About 25 minutes

Calories per serving: 347

1½ pounds monkfish fillets

2 tablespoons all-purpose flour

 Caper Sauce (recipe follows)

2 tablespoons salad oil

 Parsley sprigs

 Lemon wedges

A sauce of sautéed fresh tomatoes, onion, wine, and capers is a lively foil for the flavor of this fish, likened by some to that of lobster.

Remove and discard membrane from fish, if necessary. Rinse fish and pat dry. Cut fillets into serving-size pieces, about 1 inch thick. Sprinkle with flour, coating lightly on all sides; shake off excess.

Prepare Caper Sauce and keep warm.

Heat oil in a wide nonstick frying pan over medium-high heat. Add fish and cook, turning once, until lightly browned on both sides and opaque in center when tested with a knife (about 8 minutes *total*). Arrange fillets on a warm platter. Spoon hot sauce around fish; garnish with parsley and lemon wedges. Makes 4 servings.

Caper Sauce. Heat 1 tablespoon **salad oil** in a wide nonstick frying pan over medium-high heat; add 1 medium-size **onion,** finely chopped, and 2 medium-size **tomatoes,** seeded and chopped. Cook, stirring often, until onion is soft (about 10 minutes). Stir in ¼ cup **dry white wine** and 2 teaspoons *each* **Dijon mustard** and **drained capers;** boil, stirring, until thickened. Serve hot.

Per serving: 34 grams protein, 10 grams carbohydrates, 18 grams total fat, 8 grams unsaturated fat, 59 milligrams cholesterol, 86 milligrams sodium.

BUTTERFLIED TROUT WITH ORANGE

Preparation time: 20 minutes
Baking time: 12 to 15 minutes

Calories per serving: 321

Vegetable oil cooking spray

6 boned trout (6 to 8 oz. *each*)

1 large orange

4 tablespoons butter or margarine

3 shallots or green onions (including tops), finely chopped

3 tablespoons lemon juice

⅓ cup dry white wine or regular-strength chicken broth

¼ cup sliced almonds

Parsley sprigs

Lively with the flavors of fresh orange and lemon juices and toasted almonds, boned and butterflied trout are wonderful for company.

Coat a shallow 12- by 18-inch baking pan with cooking spray. Spread trout open and place, skin side down, in pan.

Cut 6 thin slices from center of orange; set aside. Ream juice from remaining orange sections; measure 3 tablespoons of the juice and set aside.

In a small frying pan, melt 2 tablespoons of the butter over medium heat; add shallots and cook, stirring often, until soft (about 5 minutes). Drizzle shallot mixture evenly over trout (set frying pan aside), then drizzle with the 3 tablespoons orange juice, 1 tablespoon of the lemon juice, and wine.

Bake fish, uncovered, in a 350° oven until tops look milky white (12 to 15 minutes). About 5 minutes before fish is done, heat remaining 2 tablespoons butter in frying pan over medium heat until foamy. Add almonds and stir until nuts begin to brown. Remove pan from heat and stir in remaining 2 tablespoons lemon juice. Transfer trout to a warm platter; spoon almond mixture over. Garnish with orange slices and parsley. Makes 6 servings.

Per serving: 39 grams protein, 6 grams carbohydrates, 14 grams total fat, 5 grams unsaturated fat, 134 milligrams cholesterol, 104 milligrams sodium.

CALICO STUFFED TROUT

Preparation time: 30 minutes
Baking time: 10 to 12 minutes

Calories per serving: 287

2 tablespoons salad oil

½ cup *each* finely chopped green and red bell peppers, onion, celery, and carrot

1 clove garlic, minced or pressed

½ teaspoon *each* dry basil and oregano leaves

¼ teaspoon *each* salt and pepper

2 tablespoons *each* dry white wine and white wine vinegar

6 whole trout (¾ to 1 lb. *each*), pan dressed

Vegetable oil cooking spray

Lemon wedges

A mixture of bright red and green bell peppers, carrots, celery, and onion, all finely chopped, stands in for richer bread stuffing for large whole trout. The colorful stuffing imparts fresh flavor and succulent moistness to the fish as it bakes.

Heat oil in a medium-size frying pan over medium heat; add bell peppers, onion, celery, carrot, garlic, basil, and oregano. Cook, stirring often, until onion is soft but not browned (8 to 10 minutes). Stir in salt, pepper, wine, and vinegar; continue cooking and stirring until most of the liquid has evaporated. Remove from heat.

Rinse trout and pat dry. Spray a large shallow baking pan with cooking spray. Spoon vegetable mixture evenly into cavity of each trout. Place trout, slightly apart, in baking pan. Spray top surfaces with cooking spray.

Bake, uncovered, in a 400° oven until fish flakes easily when prodded in thickest portion with a fork (10 to 12 minutes). Serve with lemon wedges. Makes 6 servings.

Per serving: 65 grams protein, 5 grams carbohydrates, 12 grams total fat, 4 grams unsaturated fat, 188 milligrams cholesterol, 111 milligrams sodium.

PARCHMENT-BAKED FISH FILLETS

Preparation time: 25 minutes
Baking time: 7 to 10 minutes

Calories per serving: 223

---

2 tablespoons butter or margarine, softened

2 teaspoons minced fresh ginger or ½ teaspoon ground ginger

1 teaspoon *each* ground cumin, ground coriander, and ground turmeric

¼ teaspoon fennel seeds, crushed

⅛ teaspoon ground red pepper (cayenne)

1½ pounds lingcod or Pacific snapper fillets (about 1 inch thick)

Vegetable oil cooking spray

2 medium-size tomatoes, seeded and finely chopped

2 green onions (including tops), thinly sliced

½ teaspoon salt

Baked fish fillets stay so moist inside easy-to-fold parchment envelopes that you don't need to add any high-calorie sauces. You can assemble each packet ahead and refrigerate them overnight. Look for the rolls of parchment paper in well-stocked supermarkets or in cookware stores.

In a small bowl, combine butter, ginger, cumin, coriander, turmeric, fennel seeds, and red pepper; stir until blended. Set mixture aside.

Cut fish into 4 equal pieces. Cut 4 sheets of cooking parchment, each about 4 times wider and 6 inches longer than fish portion. About 1 inch from edge of long side, spray each piece of parchment with cooking spray, covering an area about same size as fish. Center a piece of fish on sprayed area of each piece of parchment.

Spread each piece of fish with a fourth of the butter mixture, then top with a fourth *each* of the tomatoes and onions. Sprinkle each with ⅛ teaspoon of the salt.

For each packet, fold edge of parchment closest to fish over it, then fold forward with fish to enclose; with cut edge of parchment down, make 2 folds in parchment at each open end, pressing to crease lightly and tucking ends under to hold in place. (At this point, you may refrigerate until next day.)

Place packets slightly apart, smooth side up, on a large baking sheet. Spray packets with cooking spray. Bake in a 500° oven until fish is opaque in center (7 to 10 minutes); cut a tiny slit through parchment into fish to check.

Immediately transfer fish packets to dinner plates. To serve, cut packets down center of top with a sharp knife or scissors, then tear back parchment just enough to expose fish. Makes 4 servings.

Per serving: 34 grams protein, 3 grams carbohydrates, 7 grams total fat, 2 grams unsaturated fat, 126 milligrams cholesterol, 452 milligrams sodium.

LIGHT TOUCHES: FISH—LEAN & FAT

Though fish in general is considered a lowfat source of protein, the fat content of the different types can vary from less than 2 percent to over 10 percent.

Here's a list of some of the more familiar kinds of fish arranged by their fat content, from very low to high.

• *Very low (less than 2 percent fat):* Cod, halibut (Pacific), lingcod, rockfish, sea bass.
Average calories per 4 ounces: 105.

• *Low (2 to 5 percent fat):* Bluefish, catfish, flounder or sole, haddock, red snapper, shark, turbot (Greenland).
Average calories per 4 ounces: 117.

• *Moderate (6 to 10 percent fat):* Albacore, mullet, pompano, salmon (Pacific), swordfish, trout.
Average calories per 4 ounces: 194.

• *High (more than 10 percent fat):* Mackerel, shad, shad roe.
Average calories per 4 ounces: 205.

YUGOSLAVIAN FISH SKEWERS
(Pictured on facing page)

Preparation time: 25 minutes
Chilling time: 30 minutes or more
Cooking time: 10 to 12 minutes

Calories per serving: 239

Serbian Tomato Relish (recipe follows)

2 pounds **halibut, turbot, or lingcod steaks or fillets** (1 inch thick)

3 tablespoons **olive oil**

2 cloves **garlic, minced or pressed**

¼ teaspoon **pepper**

Vegetable oil cooking spray

This light idea from the Adriatic coast pairs grilled fish with a piquant relish of chopped fresh tomatoes, onion, and chiles.

Prepare Serbian Tomato Relish.

Cut away and discard skin and bones (if any) from fish; cut into 1½-inch chunks. In a large bowl, mix oil, garlic, and pepper; add fish pieces, turning lightly to coat on all sides. Thread onto 6 skewers.

Spray a barbecue grill with cooking spray. Place skewers on grill 4 to 6 inches above a solid bed of medium coals. Grill, turning carefully to cook on all sides, until lightly browned (10 to 12 minutes *total*). Serve with tomato relish. Makes 6 servings.

Serbian Tomato Relish. Core, peel, and dice 2 large **tomatoes.** In a medium-size bowl, combine tomatoes; 1 medium-size **onion,** finely chopped; 1 *each* small hot **red, green, and yellow chiles,** seeded and finely chopped; ¼ teaspoon **salt;** 1 teaspoon **sugar;** and 1 tablespoon **red wine vinegar.** Stir until well combined. Cover and refrigerate for at least 30 minutes or until next day. Makes about 3 cups.

Per serving: 33 grams protein, 6 grams carbohydrates, 9 grams total fat, 5 grams unsaturated fat, 48 milligrams cholesterol, 176 milligrams sodium.

FISH & VEGETABLE SKEWERS

Preparation time: 20 minutes
Marinating time: 3 hours or more
Cooking time: About 10 minutes

Calories per serving: 316

2 pounds **swordfish or other firm-textured fish steaks or fillets, such as halibut, shark, or lingcod** (1 inch thick)

Marinade (recipe follows)

2 small **zucchini, cut into ¼-inch slices**

1 large **red onion, cut into 1-inch pieces**

2 large **green or red bell peppers, seeded and cut into 1-inch pieces**

12 to 18 large **mushrooms**

Vegetable oil cooking spray

Skewer marinated chunks of fish with bright fresh vegetables, then pop them on the grill for a summer barbecue.

Cut away and discard skin and bones (if any) from fish; cut into 1- by 1½-inch chunks.

Prepare Marinade. Add fish pieces, turning lightly to coat on all sides. Cover and refrigerate for at least 3 hours or until next day, gently stirring fish once or twice.

Lift fish from marinade. Add zucchini, onion, bell peppers, and mushrooms to marinade; mix lightly, then lift out. Thread fish and vegetables onto 6 long skewers.

Spray a barbecue grill with cooking spray. Place skewers on grill 4 to 6 inches above a solid bed of hot coals. Grill, turning carefully to cook on all sides, until fish flakes when prodded with a fork (about 10 minutes *total*). Makes 6 servings.

Marinade. In a large bowl, mix ¼ cup **salad oil,** ⅓ cup **lemon juice,** 2 tablespoons minced **fresh ginger,** 1 teaspoon **soy sauce,** ¼ teaspoon **pepper,** and 1 clove **garlic,** minced or pressed.

Per serving: 33 grams protein, 12 grams carbohydrates, 16 grams total fat, 7 grams unsaturated fat, 72 milligrams cholesterol, 95 milligrams sodium.

The sizzle of the grill and the zesty flavor
of chile-tomato relish lift Yugoslavian Fish Skewers (facing page)
out of the ordinary. Chunks of halibut are coated with a garlic-olive oil mixture
and quickly grilled; offer the light and zippy relish alongside.

Fish and shellfish cooked in the microwave emerge so moist and juicy that you don't even need to add any butter or sauce.

But watch the timing carefully. Since microwave ovens vary widely in performance, treat our cooking times as guides only. Start checking for doneness at the minimum time given and allow for standing time.

Scallops with Pea Pods

Scallops and mushrooms cooked in a ginger-seasoned sauce team up with crunchy Chinese pea pods in this delicious microwave meal.

  6 **medium-size fresh or dried shiitake mushrooms (2 to 3 inches in diameter)**
  1 **green onion (including top)**
  ¾ **pound sea scallops, rinsed and sliced ¼ inch thick**
  3 **thin slices fresh ginger (*each about 1 inch in diameter*)**
  5 **teaspoons salad oil**
  4 **teaspoons soy sauce**
  2 **teaspoons dry sherry**
  ½ **pound Chinese pea pods (snow or sugar peas), ends and strings removed, rinsed**

Trim stems from fresh mushrooms and discard. Cut caps into thin slivers. (If using dry mushrooms, soak in hot water until soft, about 20 minutes; drain. Cut off and discard stems. Thinly slice caps.)

Cut onion lengthwise into thin strips, then crosswise into 1-inch pieces. Set aside about a fourth. In a shallow 1½-quart microwave-safe dish, mix remaining onion, mushrooms, scallops, ginger, oil, soy sauce, and sherry. Cover and let stand for 30 minutes, stirring occasionally.

Spread scallop mixture in an even layer in dish and cover loosely with wax paper. Microwave on **HIGH (100%)** for 3 to 5 minutes, stirring every 2 minutes, or just until scallops are opaque

throughout. Let mixture stand, covered, for 4 to 5 minutes.

Meanwhile, place peas (with water that clings to them) in a shallow 1-quart microwave-safe dish. Cover with lid or plastic wrap. Microwave on **HIGH (100%)** for about 3 minutes, stirring after 2 minutes, or just until tender. Let stand for 1 minute; then transfer to serving plates.

Remove and discard ginger slices; spoon scallop mixture beside peas. Garnish with reserved onion. Makes 2 servings. *Calories per serving:* 320.

Salmon & Cucumber Plate

Tiny potatoes, salmon, and cucumber sticks cook in sequence in a total of about 10 minutes, right on your dinner plate.

  3 **small thin-skinned potatoes (about 1½ inches in diameter)**
  2 **teaspoons butter or margarine**
  1 **small salmon steak (about 6 oz.)**
  ½ **teaspoon prepared horseradish**
  ¼ **to ½ cucumber, peeled and cut into julienne strips**

Pierce potatoes with a fork in several places or cut a strip of peel from around center. Put potatoes on one side of a microwave-safe dinner plate and dot with butter. Cover loosely with plastic wrap and microwave on **HIGH (100%)** for 4 to 6 minutes or just until soft when pierced.

Place salmon next to potatoes; cover and microwave on **HIGH (100%)** for 3 to 4 minutes, rotating plate after 1½ minutes, or just until fish is lighter pink near bone in center when tested with a knife. Turn salmon over and top with horseradish; arrange cucumber strips on plate, turning to coat with juices. Cover and microwave on **HIGH (100%)** for 40 to 50 seconds or just until cucumber is heated through. Makes 1 serving. *Calories per serving:* 445.

FRESH-TASTING FISH—THE MICROWAVE WAY

Microwaving is the perfect way to cook fish and shellfish. Why? Because a microwave cooks them in their own moisture, without extra fat, so all their fresh, natural flavor comes through. The results are moist and delectable.

MARINATED SOLE WITH VEGETABLES

Preparation time: 20 minutes
Marinating time: 4 hours or more
Cooking time: 12 to 15 minutes

Calories per serving: 189

1 pound small sole fillets

2 tablespoons lemon juice

¼ cup white wine vinegar

½ cup water

½ teaspoon *each* salt and thyme leaves

¼ teaspoon sugar

⅛ teaspoon pepper

1 bay leaf

2 tablespoons salad oil

½ teaspoon paprika

2 small carrots

2 small stalks celery

1 medium-size onion, slivered

1 clove garlic, minced or pressed

Lettuce leaves

Chopped parsley

Lemon wedges

In summer, when light eating is in order, offer this refreshing make-ahead sole entrée. Sautéed fish and fresh vegetables are bathed in a tangy marinade, then served cold on a bed of lettuce.

Sprinkle sole with lemon juice and let stand while preparing vinegar mixture. In a small bowl, mix vinegar, water, salt, thyme, sugar, pepper, and bay leaf, stirring until sugar is dissolved. Set aside.

Heat oil in a wide nonstick frying pan over medium heat. Pat fish lightly with paper towels; sprinkle evenly with paprika on both sides. Place fish in pan and cook, turning once, until fish flakes easily when prodded in thickest portion with a fork (4 to 6 minutes *total*). Arrange fish in a single layer in a shallow glass baking dish.

Cut carrots and celery into ¼- by 2-inch strips. Add carrots to pan and cook, stirring often, for 2 minutes. Add celery, onion, and garlic and cook, stirring often, for 2 more minutes. Stir in vinegar mixture; cover and simmer for 1 minute. Pour vegetables and cooking liquid over fish. Let cool, then cover and refrigerate for at least 4 hours or until next day.

Line 4 serving plates with lettuce leaves and arrange fish on top; spoon vegetables over fish. Garnish with parsley and lemon wedges. Makes 4 servings.

Per serving: 20 grams protein, 10 grams carbohydrates, 8 grams total fat, 6 grams unsaturated fat, 48 milligrams cholesterol, 392 milligrams sodium.

TUNA PIE WITH SPINACH-RICE CRUST

Preparation time: 20 minutes
Baking time: 40 to 45 minutes

Calories per serving: 194

Spinach-Rice Crust (recipe follows)

Vegetable oil cooking spray

1 can (6½ oz.) chunk light tuna packed in water, drained

1 cup (4 oz.) shredded Swiss cheese

4 green onions (including tops), thinly sliced

½ cup finely chopped red bell pepper

2 eggs

1 cup nonfat milk

½ teaspoon salt

¼ teaspoon liquid hot pepper seasoning

Tuna packed in spring water is a refreshingly light and convenient source of lowfat protein. Baked in an unusual, nutritious "crust" of rice and chopped spinach, it makes a stylish and colorful casserole.

Prepare Spinach-Rice Crust. Spray sides and bottom of a 10-inch quiche dish (or other shallow, round 6-cup baking dish) with cooking spray. Press rice mixture evenly over bottom and sides of dish. Distribute tuna over crust. Sprinkle with cheese, then with onions and bell pepper.

In a medium-size bowl, beat eggs with milk, salt, and hot pepper seasoning until well blended. Pour over vegetables.

Bake, uncovered, in a 350° oven until filling is set and top is lightly browned (40 to 45 minutes). Let stand for about 5 minutes, then cut into wedges to serve. Makes 6 servings.

Spinach-Rice Crust. Thaw 1 package (10 oz.) frozen chopped **spinach;** press or squeeze out as much moisture as possible. In a medium-size bowl, mix spinach with 1 cup cooked **rice** until well combined.

Per serving: 20 grams protein, 12 grams carbohydrates, 8 grams total fat, 3 grams unsaturated fat, 123 milligrams cholesterol, 485 milligrams sodium.

Viva the green, white, and red! Spinach pasta,
bay scallops, and red bell peppers celebrate the bright
colors of the Italian flag. Wine and just a touch of cream make a light,
rich-tasting sauce for Bandiera Italiana (page 60).

58

GRILLED SOY-LEMON HALIBUT

2 pounds halibut, shark, or sea bass steaks or fillets (¾ to 1 inch thick)

2 tablespoons butter or margarine, melted

3 tablespoons soy sauce

2 tablespoons lemon juice

1 tablespoon *each* sugar and Worcestershire

1 tablespoon minced fresh ginger or ½ teaspoon ground ginger

1 clove garlic, minced or pressed

⅛ teaspoon pepper

Vegetable oil cooking spray

Lemon wedges

n time: 10 minutes
g time: 1 to 2 hours
time: 8 to 10 minutes

iyaki marinade halibut's mild flavor, ew calories to this cious entrée.

Cut fish into serving-size pieces, if necessary. In a shallow baking dish, mix butter, soy sauce, lemon juice, sugar, Worcestershire, ginger, garlic, and pepper. Add fish, turning to coat on all sides. Cover and refrigerate for 1 to 2 hours, turning occasionally.

Spray grill of a covered barbecue with cooking spray. Place fish on grill 4 to 6 inches above a solid bed of hot coals. Cover barbecue (leave vents open) and grill fish, turning once, until fish flakes when prodded in thickest portion with a fork (8 to 10 minutes *total*). Serve with lemon wedges. Makes 6 servings.

Calories per serving: 202

Per serving: 32 grams protein, 4 grams carbohydrates, 6 grams total fat, 1 gram unsaturated fat, 60 milligrams cholesterol, 821 milligrams sodium.

CRUSTY FISH WITH YOGURT-DILL SAUCE

1 cup plain yogurt

½ teaspoon *each* dill weed and Dijon mustard

½ cup chopped green bell pepper

½ cup thinly sliced green onions (including tops)

1 egg

1 tablespoon nonfat milk

⅓ cup fine dry bread crumbs

3 tablespoons grated Parmesan cheese

1½ pounds rockfish or lingcod fillets (about 1 inch thick)

1 tablespoon salad oil

2 tablespoons butter or margarine

Preparation time: 20 minutes
Baking time: 10 minutes

Rockfish or lingcod fillets bake to golden perfection in a crisp coating of Parmesan cheese and bread crumbs. Dill-flavored yogurt sauce provides a light and tangy alternative to the traditional high-calorie tartar sauce.

In a medium-size bowl, combine yogurt, dill weed, mustard, bell pepper, and onions; stir until well combined. Set aside. If made ahead, cover and refrigerate sauce for up to a day.

Place a shallow nonstick 9- by 12-inch (or larger) baking pan in oven; preheat to 500°. Meanwhile, beat egg and milk in a shallow pan until blended; mix bread crumbs and cheese in another shallow pan or on wax paper. Cut fish into serving-size pieces, if necessary. Dip fish first into egg mixture, then into crumb mixture, coating well on all sides.

Remove baking pan from oven. Add oil and butter, swirling pan to melt butter. Arrange fish in pan in a single layer, turning to coat all over with butter mixture. Bake, uncovered, until fish is opaque in center when tested with a knife (about 10 minutes). Serve with yogurt sauce. Makes 6 servings.

Calories per serving: 246

Per serving: 25 grams protein, 10 grams carbohydrates, 12 grams total fat, 4 grams unsaturated fat, 120 milligrams cholesterol, 221 milligrams sodium.

BANDIERA ITALIANA
(Pictured on page 58)

Preparation time: 10 minutes
Cooking time: About 15 minutes

Calories per serving: 391

2	tablespoons butter or margarine
½	pound bay scallops or thinly sliced sea scallops, rinsed and patted dry
1	large red bell pepper, seeded and finely chopped
4	ounces thin dry spinach noodles
½	cup dry white wine
⅓	cup whipping cream
	Lemon wedges

The colors of the Italian flag are the inspiration for this light and creamy pasta entrée, a combination of green pasta, white scallops, and red bell pepper.

In a wide nonstick frying pan, melt 1 tablespoon of the butter over medium heat. Add scallops and cook, stirring, just until opaque (1 to 2 minutes). Remove with a slotted spoon and set aside. Melt remaining 1 tablespoon butter in pan, then stir in bell pepper and cook, stirring often, just until soft (about 5 minutes); remove with a slotted spoon and add to scallops. Set pan aside.

While pepper is cooking, cook noodles in 3 to 4 quarts boiling water in a 4- to 5-quart pan just until tender to bite (5 to 7 minutes); drain well.

To pan in which pepper was cooked, add wine and any liquid that has accumulated with scallops. Bring to a boil over high heat and cook, stirring, until liquid is reduced by about half. Stir in cream. Add noodles, mix lightly to coat with sauce, then remove from heat and stir in scallops and pepper. Serve on warm plates and garnish with lemon wedges. Makes 3 servings.

Per serving: 18 grams protein, 35 grams carbohydrates, 19 grams total fat, 7 grams unsaturated fat, 94 milligrams cholesterol, 306 milligrams sodium.

LIGHT TOUCHES: EATING LIGHT WHEN YOU'RE DINING OUT

You *can* eat light when you dine at a restaurant—it's simply a matter of knowing how to choose wisely from the menu. Often, you'll find that your best bet is naturally light fish or shellfish.

Note how the fish is cooked before you choose. Look for fish that's broiled or grilled, stir-fried, or poached or steamed.

Steer clear of rich embellishments such as tartar sauce or butter-based sauces like hollandaise, béarnaise, or beurre blanc—they can ruin your best intentions. Instead, top your fish with a fresh tomato sauce, a creamy yogurt-based sauce, or a zesty salsa, or simply a squeeze of lemon, lime, or orange.

FRYING-PAN SCALLOPS

Preparation time: 5 minutes
Cooking time: 6 to 8 minutes

Calories per serving: 234

1	tablespoon olive oil or salad oil
1	pound sea scallops or bay scallops, rinsed and patted dry
1	clove garlic, minced or pressed
2	tablespoons butter or margarine
2	tablespoons *each* lemon juice and chopped parsley

Quickly sautéed scallops need only a touch of garlic and lemon to enhance their wonderful flavor.

Place a wide nonstick frying pan over medium-high heat until a drop of water sizzles and dances in pan. Add oil, tilting pan to coat. Add scallops and garlic; cook, turning often, until scallops are lightly browned and no longer translucent in center when tested with a knife (about 5 minutes for sea scallops, 3 minutes for bay scallops). Transfer to a warm serving dish and keep warm.

Add butter to pan and swirl over medium heat until butter is foamy and begins to brown. Remove from heat and stir in lemon juice and parsley; pour over scallops. Makes 3 servings.

Per serving: 23 grams protein, 6 grams carbohydrates, 12 grams total fat, 6 grams unsaturated fat, 24 milligrams cholesterol, 481 milligrams sodium.

Fish and shellfish stay exceptionally moist and flavorful when they're steamed. Positioned on a rack in a steamer, live and raw shellfish and foil-wrapped fish are easy to handle.

You can use one of several types of steamers, such as a large metal kettle with a rack or a fish poacher made especially for whole fish, or you can improvise your own. All you need is a pan containing an inch or so of water, a device (a rack, dish, or perforated tray) to support the food above the water, and a lid to keep in the steam.

Steam-poached Fish Fillets or Steaks

Steamed in foil, this savory fish gets a crowning touch of herbed tomato sauce.

1½ pounds halibut, snapper, or lingcod fillets or steaks
6 parsley sprigs
3 thin slices onion
½ bay leaf or 3 thin slices fresh ginger
Portuguese Tomato Sauce (recipe follows)

Place fish fillets on a piece of foil large enough to enclose fish, arranging pieces in a compact, evenly thick layer. Top fish with parsley, onion, and bay leaf.

Wrap foil around fish, sealing edges securely. Place on a rack in a deep kettle over at least 1 inch of boiling water. Cover and steam until fish looks just slightly translucent in center of thickest part when tested with a knife (12 to 15 minutes for each inch of thickness). Meanwhile, prepare Portuguese Tomato Sauce.

Open foil carefully, lift out fish (discarding seasonings and juices), and arrange on a warm plate. Spoon tomato sauce over and around fish. Makes 4 servings. *Calories per serving: 240.*

MOIST & TENDER STEAMED FISH

The moist, even, gentle heat of steam cooking is ideal for fish and shellfish. No fat is needed when you cook with steam, and because steaming retains the food's natural flavor, you don't need rich sauces or butters. Try this quick and easy method with all kinds of seafood.

Portuguese Tomato Sauce. In a wide nonstick frying pan, melt 1 tablespoon **butter** or margarine over medium heat. Add 1 medium-size **onion,** thinly sliced; cook, stirring, until barely soft (3 to 5 minutes).

Add 1 large clove **garlic,** minced or pressed, 1 can (about 1 lb.) **pear-shaped tomatoes** (break up with a spoon) and their liquid, and ½ teaspoon *each* **dry basil** and **thyme leaves.** Cook, uncovered, stirring often, until reduced to about 2 cups (about 5 minutes).

Steam-poached Whole Fish

For this elegant presentation of a whole fish, use a fish poacher or roaster a little longer than the fish.

1 whole bluefish or striped bass (5 to 6 lbs.), cleaned and dressed
12 parsley sprigs
4 to 6 thin slices onion
1 bay leaf
Portuguese Tomato Sauce (see above)

Rinse fish and pat dry. Place fish on a piece of foil large enough to enclose whole fish. Place parsley, onion, and bay leaf in cavity. Wrap foil around fish, sealing edges securely.

Insert a meat thermometer through foil into thickest part of fish, parallel to but not touching backbone. Place on a rack over at least 1 inch of boiling water in a fish poacher or roaster. Cover and steam to an internal temperature of 120° or until fish looks just slightly translucent in center of thickest part when tested with a knife (12 to 15 minutes for each inch of thickness, measured in thickest part of fish). Meanwhile, prepare Portuguese Tomato Sauce.

Open foil and drain off juices. Transfer fish to a large serving plate. Accompany with tomato sauce. Makes 6 servings. *Calories per serving: 275.*

PARCHMENT-BAKED SHRIMP & PESTO
(Pictured on facing page)

🍶 *Preparation time:* 30 minutes
Baking time: 7 to 10 minutes

📏 *Calories per serving:* 244

¾	**cup lightly packed fresh basil leaves; or 2 tablespoons dry basil and ¾ cup lightly packed parsley**
⅓	**cup grated Parmesan cheese**
1	**clove garlic, minced or pressed**
3	**tablespoons** *each* **olive oil and lemon juice**
1½	**pounds jumbo shrimp, shelled and deveined**
	Vegetable oil cooking spray
4	**thin lemon slices**
4	**Niçoise or small ripe olives**
	Pepper

Top jumbo shrimp with pesto sauce and wrap in parchment for a very low-calorie entrée.

In a food processor or blender, combine basil, cheese, garlic, olive oil, and lemon juice; whirl until smoothly puréed. Set pesto aside.

Divide shrimp into 4 equal rows, overlapping shrimp in each row slightly. Cut 4 sheets of cooking parchment, each about 6 inches longer than a portion of shrimp and 4 times as wide as narrow side. About 1 inch from edge of long side, spray each piece of parchment with cooking spray, covering an area about same size as a serving of shrimp. Arrange shrimp on sprayed area of each piece of parchment.

Top each serving with a fourth of the pesto, a lemon slice, and an olive. Sprinkle lightly with pepper.

For each packet, fold edge of parchment closest to shrimp over them, then fold forward with shrimp to enclose; with cut edge of parchment down, make 2 folds in parchment at each open end, pressing to crease lightly and tucking ends under to hold in place. (At this point, you may refrigerate until next day.)

Place packets slightly apart, smooth side up, on a large baking sheet. Spray packets with cooking spray. Bake in a 500° oven until shrimp are opaque in center (7 to 10 minutes); cut a tiny slit through parchment into shrimp to check.

Immediately transfer packets to dinner plates. To serve, cut packets down center of top with a sharp knife or scissors, then tear back parchment just enough to expose filling. Makes 4 servings.

Per serving: 24 grams protein, 10 grams carbohydrates, 17 grams total fat, 10 grams unsaturated fat, 6 milligrams cholesterol, 297 milligrams sodium.

STIR-FRIED SHRIMP WITH PEKING SAUCE
(Pictured on cover)

🍶 *Preparation time:* 30 minutes
Cooking time: 6 to 8 minutes

📏 *Calories per serving:* 264

	Peking Stir-fry Sauce (recipe follows)
2	**tablespoons salad oil**
1	**pound medium-size shrimp (30 to 40 per lb.), shelled and deveined**
1	**large red onion, slivered**
2	**cups broccoli flowerets**
1	*each* **red and yellow or green bell peppers, seeded and cut into long strips**
2	**to 4 tablespoons water**
2	**teaspoons cornstarch**

Tender shrimp are tossed with a colorful mélange of vegetables to create a dish with Asian flair.

Prepare Peking Stir-fry Sauce; set aside.

Place a wok or wide nonstick frying pan over high heat. When pan is hot, add 1 tablespoon of the oil, then shrimp. Stir-fry just until shrimp are pink (about 2 minutes). Remove shrimp from pan.

To pan add remaining oil, onion, broccoli, bell peppers, and 1 tablespoon of the water. Stir-fry, adding water as needed, until broccoli is barely tender to bite (2 to 4 minutes).

Blend cornstarch into prepared sauce. Add to pan and stir just until sauce is thickened and clear. Add shrimp, stirring just until heated through. Serve immediately. Makes 4 servings.

Peking Stir-fry Sauce. In a small bowl, combine 2 cloves **garlic,** minced or pressed, 2 tablespoons minced **fresh ginger** or 1 teaspoon ground ginger, ½ cup **water,** ¼ cup **hoisin sauce,** 2 tablespoons **soy sauce,** 1 tablespoon **rice wine vinegar,** and 2 teaspoons **sugar.** Stir until well combined.

Per serving: 25 grams protein, 15 grams carbohydrates, 8 grams total fat, 6 grams unsaturated fat, 179 milligrams cholesterol, 833 milligrams sodium.

Cut open the parchment and voilà! Plump jumbo
shrimp topped with a purée of fresh basil and garlic
send up a tempting aroma. At only 244 calories, Parchment-baked Shrimp &
Pesto (facing page) is a real gift to calorie-counters.

C·H·I·C·K·E·N &

What food is delicious, economical, low in calories and saturated fats, high in protein, and adaptable enough to taste good with everything from peaches to curry spices? The answer, of course, is poultry—the ideal food for lovers of light cuisine.

Moreover, as you'll see from the recipes in this chapter, versatile poultry can be prepared in an almost infinite number of ways—from saucy stir-fries to juicy barbecues.

Wholesome temptations. It seems almost too good to be true that poultry, so delicious when prepared with imagination and flair, is also so good for you. Nutritional analysis shows that turkey and chicken are not only high in protein and low in cholesterol and calories but also boast a high ratio of polyunsaturated fats to saturated fats. Nutritionists believe this can actually help to lower blood cholesterol.

Poultry for every taste. No matter what your preference, you're sure to find a favorite in our collection. Like a hint of sweetness? Try gleaming Chutney-glazed Chicken Thighs (page 79). Looking for an intriguingly different flavor in a roasted chicken? Succulent Cilantro & Sake Roast Chicken (facing page) fits the bill. If spicy flavor is what you crave, grill up Barbecued Turkey Breast Steaks (page 82) and top them with fresh, zesty salsa.

Marinades infuse chicken parts with subtle piquancy before they're broiled or grilled. Broiled Chicken with Peaches (page 68) derives its wonderful flavor from a marinade of basil-scented raspberry vinegar; Grilled Garlic-Orange Chicken

(page 67) is enlivened by a garlicky orange-rosemary marinade. Basting poultry as it roasts or grills imparts a lively essence and a beautiful, gleaming glaze. Grilled Game Hens with Jalapeño Jelly Glaze (page 81) look as juicy and succulent as they taste.

Of course, poultry also picks up flavor when it's simmered or sautéed with herbs, spices, and other flavorings. For an unusual combination of tastes, try tender Chicken with Tangy Caper Sauce (page 69), simmered in apple juice and rum.

Ways to cook it light. It's easy to cook chicken, turkey, and other poultry to moist, tender goodness without adding unnecessary calories in the form of rich sauces or high-calorie stuffings. *Roasting* poultry with aromatic herbs tucked into the bird's cavity is one method. *Grilling* and *barbecuing* also cook chicken and turkey to perfection using little or no added fat; in fact, much of the hidden fat on the bird drips away.

Broiling is a time-honored method that's easy and light; so are *stir-frying* and *sautéing*, which have the added advantage of speed.

Finally, we offer some methods that are just a little bit different, and that make all the difference in flavor. One method, *roasting in a covered barbecue*, imparts a wonderfully smoky flavor to turkey and chicken while keeping it moist and tender. Another method, one that may be new to you, is *steeping*. It calls for gently cooking chicken and turkey parts in hot water, with results that are tender and silken in texture, as well as low in calories.

Serve it golden crisp and spicy from the grill, or as a delicate sauté. Add sweet peaches or tangy marinated vegetables. Make it plain or fancy, hot or cold. Any way you slice, dice, or split it, poultry is the food that's always at the ready when you want to cook something interesting *and* light.

T·U·R·K·E·Y

CILANTRO & SAKE ROAST CHICKEN
(Pictured on page 66)

Preparation time: 15 minutes
Baking time: 1 to 1¼ hours

Calories per serving: 225

1 frying chicken
(3½ to 4 lbs.)

Pepper

1 cup coarsely chopped celery (including leaves)

1 cup chopped fresh cilantro (coriander)

8 fresh rosemary sprigs (*each* about 2 inches long) or ¾ teaspoon dry rosemary

½ cup sake or dry sherry

Vegetable oil cooking spray

Roasted chicken takes on new character when you flavor it with an intriguing blend of cilantro, rosemary, celery, and sake. The aromatic mixture also helps keep the chicken moist as it roasts.

Remove giblets from chicken and reserve for other uses. Pull off and discard all visible fat from chicken. Rinse inside and out; pat dry, then lightly sprinkle body cavity with pepper.

In a bowl, combine celery, cilantro, rosemary, and ¼ cup of the sake; stir until blended. Stuff mixture into body cavity of chicken; use skewers to fasten skin over cavity. Pull skin over neck opening and secure to back, then tuck wings under body.

Spray a roasting rack with cooking spray; set in a shallow pan. Place chicken, breast up, on rack. Roast, uncovered, in a 375° oven, basting several times with remaining ¼ cup sake, until meat near thighbone is no longer pink when slashed (1 to 1¼ hours). Remove and discard stuffing. Lift chicken onto a warm platter or board to carve. Makes 6 servings.

Per serving: 34 grams protein, 3 grams carbohydrates, 9 grams total fat, 7 grams unsaturated fat, 152 milligrams cholesterol, 31 milligrams sodium.

POPPY SEED ROAST CHICKEN

Preparation time: 10 minutes
Baking time: 1 to 1¼ hours

Calories per serving: 317

3 tablespoons *each* red wine vinegar, salad oil, and honey

1 tablespoon *each* poppy seeds and minced onion

½ teaspoon ground mace

1 frying chicken
(3½ to 4 lbs.)

Vegetable oil cooking spray

You baste this chicken as it roasts with a gleaming honeyed glaze; save any remaining glaze to spoon over individual servings.

In a medium-size bowl, combine vinegar, oil, honey, poppy seeds, onion, and mace. Whisk until thoroughly blended.

Remove giblets from chicken and reserve for other uses. Pull off and discard all visible fat from chicken. Rinse inside and out; pat dry. Tuck wings under body.

Spray a roasting rack with cooking spray; set in a shallow pan. Place chicken, breast up, on rack. Brush chicken with some of the poppy seed mixture. Roast, uncovered, in a 375° oven, basting once or twice with more of the poppy seed mixture, until meat near thighbone is no longer pink when slashed (1 to 1¼ hours). Lift chicken onto a warm platter or board to carve. Offer any remaining poppy seed mixture at the table. Makes 6 servings.

Per serving: 34 grams protein, 9 grams carbohydrates, 16 grams total fat, 12 grams unsaturated fat, 152 milligrams cholesterol, .77 milligram sodium.

Aromatic cilantro and rosemary, plus a touch of
sake, impart succulent moistness and exceptional flavor to
Cilantro & Sake Roast Chicken (page 65) without adding calories. Oregano-scented
Herbed Carrots & Wild Rice (page 35) are the perfect flavor complement.

GRILLED GARLIC-ORANGE CHICKEN

Preparation time: 20 minutes
Marinating time: 1 hour or more
Grilling and baking time:
  About 1 hour

Calories per serving: 355

2	large cloves garlic, minced or pressed
¼	cup olive oil or salad oil
1	teaspoon grated orange peel
½	teaspoon chopped fresh rosemary leaves or ¼ teaspoon dry rosemary
2	small frying chickens (about 3 lbs. *each*), split in half
	Paprika and pepper
1	orange, thinly sliced
	Parsley sprigs

You can cook these small chicken halves in two stages: brush them with orange-scented marinade and grill them on the barbecue until golden brown; finish them later in the oven.

In a small bowl, combine garlic, oil, orange peel, and rosemary. Cover and let stand for at least a day or for up to 7 days.

Remove giblets from chicken and reserve for other uses. Pull off and discard all visible fat from chicken. Rinse and pat dry. Brush chicken pieces on all sides with garlic-oil mixture. Arrange on a large rimmed baking sheet. Cover and let stand for 1 hour or refrigerate until next day.

Sprinkle chicken lightly with paprika and pepper. Place on a barbecue grill 4 to 6 inches above a solid bed of medium-hot coals. Grill, turning once, until browned on both sides (about 25 minutes *total*).

Return chicken halves, skin side up, to baking sheet. (At this point, you may cover loosely and let stand at room temperature for up to 2 hours or refrigerate until next day.)

Bake, uncovered, in a 350° oven until breast meat is no longer pink when slashed (about 35 minutes; 45 to 50 minutes if refrigerated). Cut each chicken half into 2 pieces; arrange quarters on a platter and garnish with orange slices and parsley. Makes 8 servings.

Per serving: 43 grams protein, 2 grams carbohydrates, 18 grams total fat, 14 grams unsaturated fat, 196 milligrams cholesterol, .32 milligram sodium.

CHICKEN CACCIATORE PRESTO
(Pictured on page 71)

Preparation time: 10 minutes
Cooking time: 30 minutes

Calories per serving: 313

1	frying chicken (about 3½ lbs.), cut up
2	tablespoons olive oil or salad oil
¼	teaspoon salt
	Pepper
2	tablespoons brandy
1	small onion, finely chopped
¼	pound mushrooms, sliced
1	fresh rosemary sprig (2 to 3 inches long) or 1 teaspoon dry rosemary
1	tablespoon all-purpose flour
½	cup dry white wine
1	can (about 16 oz.) pear-shaped tomatoes

Sauté small pieces of chicken, cook up a brandied tomato sauce, and presto—cacciatore!

Remove giblets from chicken and reserve for other uses. Pull off and discard all visible fat from chicken. Rinse chicken pieces and pat dry. With a cleaver or heavy knife, cut through bones of each piece of chicken to make 2-inch pieces.

Pour oil into a wide nonstick frying pan; place over medium-high heat. When oil is hot, add thickest dark-meat pieces of chicken and cook, turning, until browned on both sides (about 5 minutes *total*). Add remaining chicken and cook, turning, until pieces are well browned on both sides and meat near thighbone is no longer pink when slashed (about 15 more minutes). Sprinkle with salt and pepper.

Add brandy; when liquid bubbles, set aflame (*not* beneath an exhaust fan or near flammable items), shaking pan until flame dies. Lift out chicken pieces. Spoon off and discard all but about 1 tablespoon of the drippings.

In pan drippings cook onion, mushrooms, and rosemary, stirring often, until onion begins to brown. Sprinkle in flour and stir until golden. Blend in wine and bring to a boil. Add tomatoes (break up with a spoon) and their liquid and bring to a simmer. Return chicken to pan and cook, stirring gently, just until heated through. Makes 6 servings.

Per serving: 35 grams protein, 7 grams carbohydrates, 14 grams total fat, 11 grams unsaturated fat, 152 milligrams cholesterol, 192 milligrams sodium.

BROILED CHICKEN WITH PEACHES

Preparation time: 15 minutes
Marinating time: 2 hours or more
Broiling time: About 30 minutes

Calories per serving: 285

1 frying chicken (about 3½ lbs.), cut up

½ cup raspberry vinegar or red wine vinegar

½ cup finely chopped fresh basil leaves or 2 tablespoons dry basil

2 tablespoons salad oil

Vegetable oil cooking spray

3 firm-ripe peaches or nectarines (*each* about 2 inches in diameter)

A wonderful raspberry vinegar–basil marinade flavors this chicken dish in a way no rich sauce can duplicate.

Remove giblets from chicken and reserve for other uses. Pull off and discard all visible fat from chicken. Rinse chicken pieces and pat dry. Place in a deep bowl.

In a medium-size bowl, combine vinegar, basil, and oil; whisk until thoroughly blended. Pour over chicken, turning to coat with marinade. Cover and refrigerate for at least 2 hours or until next day.

Spray rack of a broiler pan with cooking spray. Remove chicken from marinade, reserving marinade. Place chicken on broiler rack. Broil 4 inches below heat, turning chicken to brown evenly, for 20 minutes. Meanwhile, peel peaches, cut in half, and pit. Coat fruit with reserved marinade.

Arrange peaches on rack with chicken and return to broiler. Broil until meat near thighbone is no longer pink when slashed and peaches are heated through (about 10 more minutes). Makes 6 servings.

Per serving: 34 grams protein, 6 grams carbohydrates, 13 grams total fat, 11 grams unsaturated fat, 152 milligrams cholesterol, .7 milligram sodium.

HERBED BARBECUED CHICKEN

Preparation time: 15 minutes
Grilling time: About 40 minutes

Calories per serving: 271

2 tablespoons minced parsley

1 tablespoon minced fresh sage leaves or ½ teaspoon dry sage leaves

2 teaspoons minced fresh rosemary leaves or ½ teaspoon dry rosemary

1½ teaspoons minced fresh oregano leaves or ¼ teaspoon dry oregano leaves

1 teaspoon minced fresh thyme leaves or ¼ teaspoon dry thyme leaves

1 large clove garlic, minced or pressed

2 tablespoons olive oil or salad oil

2 tablespoons *each* soy sauce and Worcestershire

¼ teaspoon pepper

1 frying chicken (about 3½ lbs.), cut up

A savory mixture of fresh herbs, brushed liberally over chicken pieces as they grill, adds irresistible flavor and aroma—and next to no calories.

In a small bowl, combine parsley, sage, rosemary, oregano, thyme, garlic, oil, soy sauce, Worcestershire, and pepper; set aside.

Remove giblets from chicken and reserve for other uses. Pull off and discard all visible fat from chicken. Rinse chicken pieces and pat dry.

Place on a barbecue grill 4 to 6 inches above a solid bed of medium coals. Grill, turning, until chicken is browned on both sides and meat near thighbone is no longer pink when slashed (35 to 40 minutes). About 5 minutes before chicken is done, brush liberally all over with herb mixture. Spoon any remaining herb mixture over individual servings. Makes 6 servings.

Per serving: 34 grams protein, 1 gram carbohydrates, 13 grams total fat, 11 grams unsaturated fat, 152 milligrams cholesterol, 506 milligrams sodium.

CHICKEN WITH HAPPY SPICES

Preparation time: 15 minutes
Cooking time: About 45 minutes

Calories per serving: 291

1 frying chicken (about 3½ lbs.), cut up

2 tablespoons butter or margarine

3 large onions, finely chopped

2 cloves garlic, minced or pressed

1 teaspoon minced fresh ginger or ½ teaspoon ground ginger

1 teaspoon ground turmeric

4 whole cardamom, pods removed and seeds crushed

5 whole cloves

1 cinnamon stick (2 inches long)

¼ teaspoon *each* chili powder and salt

A "happy" combination of aromatic seasonings lends an exotic touch to the lean, onion-rich sauce for this chicken dish.

Remove giblets from chicken and reserve for other uses. Pull off and discard all visible fat from chicken. Rinse chicken pieces and pat dry.

In a wide nonstick frying pan, melt butter over medium heat. Add chicken pieces, skin side down. Cover and cook, shaking pan often, until well browned (about 10 minutes). Turn chicken, cover, and cook until browned (about 5 more minutes). Lift out breast pieces.

Stir in onions, garlic, ginger, turmeric, cardamom seeds, cloves, cinnamon, and chili powder. Cover and cook over low heat for 15 minutes. Return breast pieces to pan, cover, and continue simmering, shaking pan occasionally, until meat in thickest portion is no longer pink when slashed (about 10 more minutes).

Transfer chicken to a warm platter and keep warm. Skim off and discard fat from pan juices. Stir in salt. To thicken sauce, if necessary, boil liquid over high heat, uncovered, for 1 to 2 minutes. Spoon sauce over chicken. Makes 6 servings.

Per serving: 35 grams protein, 8 grams carbohydrates, 13 grams total fat, 8 grams unsaturated fat, 164 milligrams cholesterol, 146 milligrams sodium.

CHICKEN WITH TANGY CAPER SAUCE

Preparation time: 10 minutes
Cooking time: About 45 minutes

Calories per serving: 317

1 frying chicken (about 3½ lbs.), cut up

2 tablespoons all-purpose flour

1 teaspoon ground ginger

½ teaspoon pepper

2 tablespoons butter or margarine

1 large onion, finely chopped

1 clove garlic, minced or pressed

1½ cups unsweetened apple juice or cider

3 tablespoons *each* lemon juice and dark rum

2 tablespoons drained capers

An unusual tart-sweet sauce made with apple juice and rum imparts rich flavor to this tender simmered chicken.

Remove giblets from chicken and reserve for other uses. Pull off and discard all visible fat from chicken. Rinse chicken pieces and pat dry. Dust with flour, shaking off excess. Sprinkle with ginger and pepper.

In a wide nonstick frying pan, melt butter over medium-high heat. Add chicken pieces, half at a time, and cook, turning, until browned on both sides (10 to 15 minutes). Remove chicken pieces as they brown and set aside.

Spoon off and discard all but about 1 tablespoon of the drippings. To pan add onion and garlic; cook, stirring often, until onion is soft (about 5 minutes). Blend in apple juice, lemon juice, rum, and capers. Return chicken to pan; cover, reduce heat to medium-low, and simmer until meat near thighbone is no longer pink when slashed (30 to 35 minutes).

Transfer chicken to a warm platter and keep warm. Skim off and discard fat from pan juices. Bring to a boil over high heat, stirring until slightly thickened. Spoon sauce over chicken. Makes 6 servings.

Per serving: 34 grams protein, 13 grams carbohydrates, 13 grams total fat, 8 grams unsaturated fat, 164 milligrams cholesterol, 51 milligrams sodium.

CHICKEN WITH SPINACH & TOMATOES

Preparation time: About 30 minutes
Cooking time: About 30 minutes

Calories per serving: 509

1	tablespoon coriander seeds
1	teaspoon whole black peppercorns
¼	cup water
6	cloves garlic
1	piece peeled fresh ginger (1 by 2 inches), cut into quarters
¼	cup salad oil
3	whole chicken breasts (3 lbs. *total*), split, skinned, and boned
2	large onions, finely chopped
⅛	teaspoon ground red pepper (cayenne)
1	large can (1 lb. 12 oz.) tomatoes
1½	pounds spinach
4	cups hot cooked rice

Garlicky chicken breasts rest on a fluffy bed of rice; present the lightly simmered vegetables alongside.

In a blender, combine coriander seeds and peppercorns; whirl until finely ground (about 2 minutes). Add water, garlic, and ginger; whirl until smooth (about 1 minute), stopping motor once or twice to scrape sides of container. Set mixture aside.

Heat 2 tablespoons of the oil in a 4- to 5-quart pan over medium-high heat. Add chicken and cook, turning, until lightly browned on both sides; remove from pan and set aside. To pan add remaining 2 tablespoons oil, then onions; cook, stirring occasionally, until onions are soft (6 to 8 minutes). Add coriander mixture and red pepper; cook, stirring, for about 30 seconds.

Spoon off and discard any excess oil. Stir in tomatoes (break up with a spoon) and their liquid. Return chicken to pan; reduce heat, cover,

and simmer until meat in thickest portion is just slightly pink when slashed (about 8 minutes).

Meanwhile, rinse spinach well, drain, and discard coarse stems. Reserve several large leaves. Coarsely chop remaining leaves. Add chopped spinach to pan, cover, and cook over medium heat, stirring often, just until spinach wilts and chicken in thickest portion is no longer pink when slashed (about 5 minutes).

With a slotted spoon, transfer spinach and tomatoes to a bowl; keep warm. Line a platter with reserved spinach leaves. Spoon rice over, then chicken; keep warm.

Bring remaining liquid in pan to a boil over high heat; cook, stirring, until reduced to about ¾ cup. Spoon sauce over chicken. Serve with spinach and tomatoes. Makes 6 servings.

Per serving: 46 grams protein, 49 grams carbohydrates, 14 grams total fat, 7 grams unsaturated fat, 120 milligrams cholesterol, 770 milligrams sodium.

ASPARAGUS CHICKEN STIR-FRY

Preparation time: 20 minutes
Cooking time: About 5 minutes

Calories per serving: 317

3	chicken breast halves (1½ lbs. *total*)
8	green onions (including tops)
1	pound asparagus
½	pound mushrooms
1	tablespoon *each* cornstarch, dry sherry, and soy sauce
½	cup regular-strength chicken broth
3	tablespoons sesame oil or salad oil
1	tablespoon minced fresh ginger or ½ teaspoon ground ginger
2	cloves garlic, minced or pressed

Because this Chinese-style dish cooks so quickly, you'll need to have all the ingredients prepared and at the ready before you start to stir-fry.

Skin and bone chicken; cut into ½- by 1-inch strips. Cut onions diagonally into 1-inch pieces. Snap off and discard tough ends of asparagus; cut diagonally into 1-inch pieces. Thinly slice mushrooms. In a small bowl, combine cornstarch, sherry, soy sauce, and broth; stir until cornstarch is dissolved.

Heat oil in a wide nonstick frying pan or wok over high heat. Add ginger, garlic, and chicken; stir-fry until chicken is white in center when slashed (about 2 minutes). With a

slotted spoon, lift chicken from pan and set aside.

To pan add mushrooms, onions, and asparagus; stir-fry for 1 minute. Add chicken and broth mixture. Bring to a boil, stirring, and cook for 1 more minute. Serve immediately. Makes 4 servings.

Per serving: 34 grams protein, 14 grams carbohydrates, 14 grams total fat, 8 grams unsaturated fat, 2 milligrams cholesterol, 433 milligrams sodium.

Cook up an Italian family favorite with speed
and style. For Chicken Cacciatore Presto (page 67), you
simmer small, quick-cooking chicken pieces in a light tomato-mushroom
sauce; serve on a bed of tender Matchstick Zucchini (page 36).

SESAME CHICKEN

Preparation time: 20 minutes
Marinating time: 1 to 2 hours
Baking time: 8 to 10 minutes

Calories per serving: 338

¼	cup soy sauce
1	tablespoon *each* sugar and dry sherry
1	tablespoon minced fresh ginger or ½ teaspoon ground ginger
2	cloves garlic, minced or pressed
3	whole chicken breasts (3 lbs. *total*), split, skinned, and boned
1	egg
¼	cup *each* all-purpose flour and sesame seeds
2	tablespoons butter or margarine
1	tablespoon salad oil

Sesame seeds make a crusty coating for juicy marinated chicken breasts; serve them with stir-fried Chinese pea pods.

In a large bowl, combine soy sauce, sugar, sherry, ginger, and garlic; stir until sugar is dissolved. Add chicken, turning to coat lightly with marinade. Cover and refrigerate for 1 to 2 hours.

Place a shallow 10- by 15-inch baking pan in oven while it preheats to 500°. In a shallow bowl, beat egg with 2 tablespoons of the marinade. Mix flour and sesame seeds on wax paper. Lift chicken pieces from remaining marinade and dip first in egg mixture, then in sesame seed mixture, turning to coat lightly on all sides.

When pan is hot, add butter and oil to pan, swirling to melt butter. Add chicken pieces, turning to coat lightly on all sides. Bake, uncovered, for 5 minutes; turn chicken pieces and continue to bake until meat in thickest portion is no longer pink when slashed (3 to 5 more minutes). Makes 6 servings.

Per serving: 41 grams protein, 9 grams carbohydrates, 15 grams total fat, 6 grams unsaturated fat, 54 milligrams cholesterol, 946 milligrams sodium.

LIGHT TOUCHES: WHEN TO SKIN THE BIRD

One of the most tempting parts of a chicken or other type of poultry is its crisp, crunchy, crackling skin. But it's also the part that contains fat—and calories. When do you leave it on, and when should you take it off?

When you roast or grill, it's best to leave the skin on, since it keeps the bird moist. If you wish, you can remove it later. When you simmer or bake poultry pieces in a moist sauce or coating, they can be skinned and still retain their succulent moistness.

Note: The nutritional totals in our recipes were calculated including skin, unless otherwise specified.

GRILLED ASIAN CHICKEN

Preparation time: 15 minutes
Marinating time: 4 hours or more
Grilling time: 20 to 30 minutes

Calories per serving: 307

6	cloves garlic, minced or pressed
⅓	cup chopped fresh cilantro (coriander)
2	teaspoons whole black peppercorns, coarsely crushed
2	teaspoons soy sauce
1	teaspoon sugar
5	tablespoons salad oil
3	pounds chicken breasts or thighs
1	tablespoon white wine vinegar

A zippy paste of cilantro, garlic, soy sauce, and peppercorns gives grilled chicken breasts an Oriental flavor.

In a blender or food processor, combine garlic, cilantro, peppercorns, soy sauce, sugar, and ¼ cup of the salad oil; whirl until a paste forms. Set aside 1½ tablespoons of the seasoning paste.

Spread remaining paste evenly over chicken (slip some under skin, if desired). Cover and refrigerate for at least 4 hours or until next day.

Place chicken pieces on a barbecue grill 4 to 6 inches above a solid bed of hot coals. Grill, turning, until chicken is evenly browned and meat is no longer pink when slashed (20 to 30 minutes). Transfer chicken to a serving platter.

Mix reserved seasoning paste with vinegar and remaining 1 tablespoon oil. Spoon over chicken. Makes 6 servings.

Per serving: 38 grams protein, 2 grams carbohydrates, 16 grams total fat, 9 grams unsaturated fat, 120 milligrams cholesterol, 147 milligrams sodium.

LEMON BASIL CHICKEN

Preparation time: 15 minutes
Cooking time: About 25 minutes

Calories per serving: 306

4 **tablespoons butter or margarine**

2 **whole chicken breasts (2 lbs. *total*), split, skinned, and boned**

1 **cup regular-strength chicken broth**

2 **teaspoons grated lemon peel**

3 **tablespoons chopped fresh basil leaves or 1 tablespoon dry basil**

2 **tablespoons lemon juice**

Fresh basil leaves (optional)

Surround boneless chicken breasts with a lemony basil sauce for a simply delicious light entrée.

In a wide nonstick frying pan, melt 1 tablespoon of the butter over medium-high heat. Add chicken and cook, turning, until lightly browned on both sides (about 3 minutes *total*). Add broth, lemon peel, chopped basil, and lemon juice. Reduce heat, cover, and simmer just until meat in thickest portion is no longer pink when slashed (10 to 12 minutes). Transfer chicken to a warm platter and keep warm.

Bring cooking liquid to a boil over high heat; boil until reduced by about two-thirds. Add any accumulated juices from chicken, then (in one chunk) remaining 3 tablespoons butter. Stir constantly until butter is melted. If sauce is too thin to coat a spoon, reduce heat slightly and boil gently, shaking and swirling pan constantly, until sauce thickens. Pour around chicken. Garnish with basil leaves, if desired. Makes 4 servings.

Per serving: 38 grams protein, 1 gram carbohydrates, 16 grams total fat, 4 grams unsaturated fat, 39 milligrams cholesterol, 321 milligrams sodium.

CHICKEN WITH A POCKETFUL OF MUSHROOMS

Preparation time: 30 minutes
Cooking time: About 20 minutes

Calories per serving: 312

Sautéed Mushrooms (recipe follows)

3 **whole chicken breasts (3 lbs. *total*), split, skinned, and boned**

6 **large fresh or dried shiitake mushrooms or large fresh mushrooms**

2 **tablespoons butter or margarine**

½ **teaspoon minced fresh ginger or ⅛ teaspoon ground ginger**

⅓ **cup dry sherry or sake**

1 **cup regular-strength chicken broth**

1½ **tablespoons soy sauce**

½ **teaspoon *each* sugar and vinegar**

1 **tablespoon cornstarch**

2 **tablespoons water**

Gingery sautéed mushrooms add delightful flavor when tucked into pockets in chicken breasts.

Prepare Sautéed Mushrooms and set aside. Gently pull off slim fillet on inside of each chicken breast half; set aside. In thickest part of each remaining breast half, cut a pocket about 3½ inches long and 2 inches deep.

Tuck 2 to 3 tablespoons of the cooked mushroom mixture into each breast pocket, packing lightly. (At this point, you may cover and refrigerate until next day.)

If using dried mushrooms, soak in hot water until soft (about 20 minutes); drain. Cut off and discard stems.

In a wide nonstick frying pan, melt butter over medium-high heat. Add chicken fillets and as many stuffed breasts as will fit in pan without crowding. Cook, turning, until browned on both sides; remove chicken pieces as they brown and set aside. Brown remaining stuffed breasts and whole mushrooms.

Add ginger, sherry, broth, soy sauce, sugar, vinegar, and all stuffed

breasts. Cover and simmer for 7 minutes. Carefully turn stuffed pieces and add fillets. Cover and simmer until meat in thickest portion is no longer pink in center (about 3 more minutes). With a slotted spoon, lift out chicken and mushrooms and place on a warm platter; keep warm.

Blend cornstarch and water; stir into pan juices. Bring to a boil over high heat, stirring; add any accumulated juices from chicken. Thin sauce with water, if necessary. Spoon over chicken. Makes 6 servings.

Sautéed Mushrooms. Finely chop ½ pound **fresh shiitake or large mushrooms.** In a wide frying pan, melt 2 tablespoons **butter** or margarine over medium heat. Add mushrooms, 1 medium-size **onion**, finely chopped, ½ teaspoon minced **fresh ginger** or ⅛ teaspoon ground ginger, and 1 clove **garlic,** minced or pressed. Stir until mushrooms and onion are very soft and all liquid has evaporated. Stir in 1 teaspoon **soy sauce.**

Per serving: 40 grams protein, 10 grams carbohydrates, 12 grams total fat, 3 grams unsaturated fat, 26 milligrams cholesterol, 625 milligrams sodium.

CHICKEN & GARLIC STIR-FRY

⅓ cup Garlic or Shallot Pickles, drained (recipe follows)

Sauce Mixture (recipe follows)

1 whole chicken breast (about 1 lb.), split, skinned, and boned

2 tablespoons salad oil

4 green onions (including tops), cut into 2-inch lengths

The surprise ingredient here is pickled garlic or shallots. The pickles are also good in salads; try the liquid as a dressing.

A day ahead, prepare Garlic or Shallot Pickles and refrigerate.

Prepare Sauce Mixture; set aside.

Cut chicken into ¼- by 3-inch strips. Place a wok or wide nonstick frying pan over high heat. When pan is hot, add oil, tilting pan to coat well. Add chicken and stir-fry until lightly browned (about 2 minutes). Add green onions and Sauce Mixture; cook, stirring, until sauce boils and thickens. Stir in the ⅓ cup pickled garlic. Serve immediately. Makes 3 servings.

Garlic or Shallot Pickles. Peel 3 cups (about 1 lb.) cloves **garlic** or small shallots. (Cut any thicker than ¾ inch in half lengthwise.)

In a 2- to 3-quart pan, combine 1½ cups **distilled white vinegar,** ⅓ cup **sugar,** and ½ teaspoon **salt.** Bring to a boil over high heat, stirring until sugar is dissolved. Drop garlic into boiling vinegar mixture and cook, uncovered, stirring occasionally, for 1 minute. Let cool.

Place pickles and their liquid in a jar, cover tightly, and refrigerate for at least a day or for up to 2 months. Makes about 1½ pints.

Sauce Mixture. In a small bowl, combine ½ cup regular-strength **chicken broth,** 2 teaspoons **cornstarch,** and 1 tablespoon *each* **soy sauce** and liquid from garlic pickles. Stir until cornstarch is dissolved.

Per serving: 27 grams protein, 20 grams carbohydrates, 12 grams total fat, 7 grams unsaturated fat, 2 milligrams cholesterol, 685 milligrams sodium.

ORIENTAL BROILED CHICKEN

Preparation time: 10 minutes
Marinating time: 20 minutes or more
Broiling time: 35 to 40 minutes

Calories per serving: 227

⅓ cup soy sauce

¼ cup dry sherry

3 tablespoons sugar

2 tablespoons prepared horseradish

2 tablespoons finely chopped onion

1½ tablespoons minced fresh ginger or 1½ teaspoons ground ginger

6 whole chicken legs, thighs attached (about 3 lbs. *total*)

Vegetable oil cooking spray

Simplicity is the key to this chicken dish, marinated in a zesty ginger-accented mixture, then broiled.

In a 1-quart or smaller pan, combine soy sauce, sherry, sugar, horseradish, onion, and ginger. Stir over low heat until sugar is dissolved; remove from heat and set aside.

Place chicken in a shallow bowl or rectangular baking dish. Pour soy sauce mixture over chicken and let stand for at least 20 minutes, turning chicken once or twice. (At this point, you may cover and refrigerate until next day.)

Spray rack of a 12- by 15-inch broiler pan with cooking spray. Remove chicken from marinade and drain briefly; reserve marinade. Place chicken pieces on broiler rack. Broil 6

inches below heat, turning chicken to brown evenly, until meat near thigh-bone is no longer pink when slashed (35 to 40 minutes); brush often during cooking with reserved marinade. If desired, skim and discard fat from drippings and serve with chicken as a sauce. Makes 6 servings.

Per serving: 29 grams protein, 9 grams carbohydrates, 17 grams total fat, 8 grams unsaturated fat, 156 milligrams cholesterol, 1174 milligrams sodium.

Sesame-sprinkled Garlic Chicken & Grapes
(page 77) looks pretty as a picture surrounded by light and luscious
red grapes, broccoli, and sliced new potatoes. Completing the colorful tableau—
refreshing Greens with Oranges (page 21).

Steeped Turkey with Curry Mayonnaise

A large turkey breast needs some direct heat before steeping.

- 1 **turkey breast half (2½ to 3 lbs.)**
- 3 **or 4 parsley sprigs**
  Curry Mayonnaise (recipe follows)
  Lettuce leaves

Place turkey in a 6- to 8-quart pan. Pour in enough water to cover turkey by 1 to 2 inches. Lift out turkey. Add parsley, cover pan, and bring water to a rolling boil over high heat. Add turkey, cover, and immediately turn heat to very low. Cook for 20 minutes. Remove from heat (do *not* uncover); let steep for 1 to 1½ hours.

Prepare Curry Mayonnaise.

Remove turkey from pan; turkey is done when meat in thickest portion is no longer pink when slashed. If not done, cover turkey. Then cover pan, bring water to a simmer, and remove from heat. Add turkey, cover, and steep until done. Drain, cool in ice water, and drain again; pat dry.

Skin and bone turkey; thinly slice across grain. Arrange lettuce and turkey on a large platter; offer mayonnaise alongside. Makes 12 servings. *Calories per serving: 325.*

Curry Mayonnaise. Heat 3 tablespoons **salad oil** in a wide frying pan over medium heat. Add 1 large **onion,** minced, 4 cloves **garlic,** minced or pressed, and 2 teaspoons minced **fresh ginger.** Cook, stirring, until onion is very soft. Add 2 teaspoons **ground coriander,** 1 teaspoon **ground cumin,** ½ teaspoon **ground turmeric,** and ¼ teaspoon **ground red pepper** (cayenne). Cook, stirring, for 1 more minute; let cool slightly.

In a blender or food processor, whirl onion mixture, 1 **egg,** ¼ cup **white wine vinegar,** 3 tablespoons **golden raisins,** and ¼ teaspoon **salt** until puréed. With motor on high, add ½ cup **salad oil** in a thin stream, whirling until thick. If made ahead, cover and refrigerate. Makes about 1⅓ cups (about 74 calories per tablespoon).

Steeped Chicken with Basil Dressing

Serve this chicken refreshingly cold with a light basil dressing.

- 2 **whole chicken breasts (2 lbs. *total*), split**
- 2 **or 3 thin lemon slices**
  Basil Dressing (recipe follows)
  Lettuce leaves
- 3 **large tomatoes, thinly sliced**

Place chicken in a wide 4- to 5-quart pan. Pour in enough water to cover chicken by 1 to 2 inches. Lift out chicken. Add lemon slices, cover pan, and bring water to a rolling boil over high heat. Remove from heat and quickly immerse chicken. Cover pan tightly and let steep for 20 minutes; do *not* uncover until time is up. Chicken is done when meat in thickest portion is no longer pink when slashed. If not done, return to pan, cover, and let steep until done.

Drain chicken, cool in ice water, and drain again; pat dry. Skin and bone chicken; slice across grain about ½ inch thick.

Prepare Basil Dressing. Arrange lettuce, tomatoes, and chicken on a serving plate; drizzle with some of the dressing. Offer remaining dressing at the table. Makes 4 servings. *Calories per serving: 353.*

Basil Dressing. In a blender or food processor, combine 1 cup lightly packed **fresh basil leaves** (or 3 tablespoons dry basil and ¼ cup chopped parsley), 2 cloves **garlic,** ¼ cup **white wine vinegar,** ¼ cup **olive oil** or salad oil, 2 tablespoons grated **Parmesan cheese,** and ⅛ teaspoon **pepper;** whirl until puréed.

STEEPING— THE GENTLE WAY TO POACH POULTRY

In this simple adaptation of a classic Chinese cooking method, poultry is cooked in a tightly covered pan of very hot liquid with little or no direct heat from the stove. The poultry gently steeps in the residual heat and emerges especially succulent and smooth-textured.

GARLIC CHICKEN & GRAPES
(Pictured on page 75)

Preparation time: 10 minutes
Baking time: About 45 minutes

Calories per serving: 267

	Vegetable oil cooking spray
6	whole chicken legs, thighs attached (about 3 lbs. *total*)
3	tablespoons *each* Dijon mustard and soy sauce
2	tablespoons *each* honey and white wine vinegar
2	cloves garlic, minced or pressed
1	tablespoon sesame seeds
2	cups red or green seedless grapes (about ¾ lb.)
	Watercress sprigs

Easy to prepare, these sesame-sprinkled chicken legs with luscious red grapes make a dramatic dinner presentation.

Spray a 9- by 13-inch baking pan with cooking spray. Place chicken legs in pan, skin side down. Cover with foil and bake in a 400° oven for 25 minutes.

While chicken is baking, combine mustard, soy sauce, honey, vinegar, and garlic in a small bowl; stir until well combined. Uncover chicken and turn skin side up. Pour mustard mixture over chicken and sprinkle with sesame seeds.

Return to oven and bake, uncovered, until meat near thighbone is no longer pink when slashed (about 15 minutes). Sprinkle grapes around chicken and bake just until grapes are heated through (3 to 5 more minutes).

Arrange chicken and grapes on a serving platter and spoon sauce over. Garnish with watercress. Makes 6 servings.

Per serving: 30 grams protein, 17 grams carbohydrates, 17 grams total fat, 8 grams unsaturated fat, 156 milligrams cholesterol, 760 milligrams sodium.

GRILLED CHICKEN WITH BAY LEAVES

Preparation time: 20 minutes
Marinating time: 6 hours or more
Grilling time: 25 to 30 minutes

Calories per serving: 343

12	chicken thighs (about 3 lbs. *total*)
3	tablespoons *each* Dijon mustard and white wine vinegar
¼	cup olive oil
1	teaspoon coarsely ground pepper
	About 3 dozen fresh bay leaves, washed, or dry bay leaves soaked in hot water for 1 hour
	About 4 medium-size crookneck squash, cut into ½-inch-thick slices
3	cups cherry tomatoes

Skewers of marinated chicken, yellow crookneck squash, and cherry tomatoes grill side by side in this whole-meal offering.

Place chicken thighs in a heavy plastic bag in a 9- by 13-inch pan.

In a small bowl, combine mustard, vinegar, oil, and pepper; stir until well combined. Pour mustard mixture over chicken. Tuck 6 of the bay leaves between chicken pieces. Seal bag securely, then turn to coat all chicken pieces with marinade. Refrigerate for at least 6 hours or until next day, turning bag once.

Remove chicken from bag, reserving marinade. Add squash to marinade in bag, turning to coat.

You will need 9 metal skewers at least 10 inches long. On each of 3 skewers, alternate 4 chicken thighs with bay leaves (include those used in marinade).

On each of 3 more skewers, thread bay leaves with 6 to 8 squash slices, piercing them from edge to edge. On each of the remaining 3 skewers, alternate a third of the tomatoes with remaining bay leaves.

Place skewers of chicken on a barbecue grill 4 to 6 inches above a solid bed of medium coals. Grill, turning often, for 10 minutes. Lay squash skewers on grill. Grill chicken and squash, turning for even heating, until meat near thighbone is no longer pink when slashed and squash is browned (15 to 20 more minutes). During last 5 minutes of cooking, place skewers of tomatoes on grill; grill, turning, just until heated through. Makes 6 servings.

Per serving: 33 grams protein, 9 grams carbohydrates, 19 grams total fat, 8 grams unsaturated fat, 156 milligrams cholesterol, 102 milligrams sodium.

Here's a light menu served up southwestern
style. It starts with crisp jicama slices dipped in lime juice
and chili powder; next comes juicy Grilled Game Hens with Jalapeño Jelly
Glaze (page 81) and, alongside, cooling Cilantro Slaw (page 21).

CHUTNEY-GLAZED CHICKEN THIGHS

Preparation time: 3 minutes
Baking time: About 40 minutes

Calories per serving: 340

Vegetable oil cooking spray

8 chicken thighs (about 2 lbs. *total*)

⅓ cup Major Grey's or other chutney, chopped

What could be simpler than chicken baked with a fruity chutney glaze? Add a curried rice pilaf with peas, and you've got supper.

Spray a 12- by 15-inch baking pan with cooking spray. Arrange chicken pieces, skin side up, in pan. Bake, uncovered, in a 400° oven until meat near thighbone is no longer pink when slashed (about 35 minutes). Brush evenly with chutney. Return

to oven and bake just until glaze is set (about 5 more minutes). Makes 4 servings.

Per serving: 30 grams protein, 14 grams carbohydrates, 19 grams total fat, 110 milligrams cholesterol, 144 milligrams sodium.

MEDITERRANEAN CHICKEN & PASTA

Preparation time: About 20 minutes
Cooking time: 10 to 15 minutes

Calories per serving: 399

3 tablespoons pine nuts

2 tablespoons olive oil or salad oil

1 large onion, finely chopped

2 cloves garlic, minced or pressed

1½ teaspoons *each* dry basil and oregano leaves

¼ to ½ teaspoon crushed red pepper

2 small zucchini (about ½ lb. *total*), cut into ⅛-inch-thick slices

½ pound mushrooms, thinly sliced

2 medium-size tomatoes, seeded and chopped

1 cup skinned and shredded cooked chicken or turkey

6 ounces dry fettuccine or other medium-wide long egg noodles

¼ cup grated Parmesan or Romano cheese

Traditional pasta dishes, such as Chicken Tetrazzini, rely on lavish use of butter and cream for a sumptuous sauce. But ours derives its tempting flavors from fresh vegetables, garlic, herbs, and pine nuts. It's colorful, innovative, *and* light!

In a medium-size frying pan, toast nuts over medium heat, shaking pan often, until golden (3 to 5 minutes). Set aside.

Heat 1 tablespoon of the oil in a wide nonstick frying pan over medium-high heat. Add onion, garlic, basil, oregano, and red pepper. Cook, stirring, until onion is soft (about 4 minutes). Add remaining oil, then zucchini, mushrooms, and tomatoes; cook, stirring, for 3 minutes. Add chicken and cook, stirring, just until heated through (about 1 more minute).

While vegetables are cooking, cook fettuccine in 4 to 5 quarts boiling water in a 5- to 6-quart pan just until pasta is tender to bite (8 to 10 minutes or following package directions); drain well.

Pour pasta onto a rimmed platter or into a shallow bowl. Spoon chicken

sauce over pasta and mix, lifting with 2 forks. Sprinkle with toasted nuts and cheese. Makes 4 servings.

Per serving: 24 grams protein, 43 grams carbohydrates, 15 grams total fat, 10 grams unsaturated fat, 72 milligrams cholesterol, 77 milligrams sodium.

Barbecue-roasted Chicken

This chicken has a wonderfully deep, smoky flavor. If you use a 6- to 7-pound roasting chicken instead of a fryer, cook it for 1½ to 1¾ hours.

1 frying chicken (3½ to 4 lbs.)
  Freshly ground pepper
  Lemon wedges (optional)
  Parsley sprigs (optional)
  Vegetable oil cooking spray

Remove giblets from chicken and reserve for other uses. Pull off and discard all visible fat from chicken. Rinse inside and out; pat dry, then sprinkle body cavity with pepper. Place lemon and parsley in cavity, if desired. Use skewers to fasten skin over cavity, if stuffed. Tuck wings under body.

Open or remove lid from a covered barbecue, then open bottom dampers. Pile about 50 long-burning briquets on fire grate; ignite briquets and let burn until hot (about 30 minutes). Using long-handled tongs, bank about half the briquets on each side of fire grate; place a metal drip pan in center.

Place cooking grill 4 to 6 inches above pan; spray grill with cooking spray.

Spray chicken lightly with cooking spray. Insert a meat thermometer in thickest part of thigh without touching bone. Set chicken, breast up, on grill directly above drip pan.

Cover barbecue and adjust dampers as necessary to maintain an even heat. Add 5 or 6 briquets to each side of fire grate at 30-minute intervals, if necessary. Cook until thermometer registers 185° F or until meat near thighbone is no longer pink when slashed (1 to 1¼ hours).

Discard stuffing, if used, and transfer chicken to a warm platter or board. Makes 6 servings. *Calories per serving: 222.*

ROASTING ON THE BARBECUE— A FLAVOR BONUS

When you roast a chicken or turkey in a covered barbecue over a charcoal fire, the bird takes on quite a different character from one that's oven roasted. The skin is crackling crisp, and the meat beneath has an appealing smoky flavor— all without any extra calories. Smoke cooking also imparts a reddish tinge to light-colored poultry that you may mistake for underdoneness—so always use a meat thermometer to check.

Barbecued Turkey

The turkey left over after the first meal is delicious served cold.

1 turkey (20 to 22 lbs.), thawed if frozen
2 teaspoons poultry seasoning
¼ teaspoon pepper
1 cup port
1 large onion, quartered
2 large carrots, cut into chunks
2 stalks celery, cut into chunks
1 clove garlic, quartered
  Vegetable oil cooking spray
3 or 4 fresh rosemary sprigs (*each* 3 to 4 inches long)

Remove giblets from turkey and reserve for other uses. Pull off and discard all visible fat from turkey. Rinse inside and out; pat dry.

In a small bowl, combine poultry seasoning and pepper. Sprinkle some into cavities; rub remaining mixture over skin. Set turkey breast down and spoon 1 to 2 tablespoons of the port into neck cavity; fasten skin over opening. Turn turkey; place onion, carrots, celery, and garlic in body cavity.

Prepare barbecue as for Barbecue-roasted Chicken. Spray turkey lightly with cooking spray. Insert a meat thermometer in thickest part of thigh without touching bone. Set turkey, breast up, on grill directly above drip pan. Pour about ⅓ cup of the remaining port into body cavity, then barbecue as directed for Barbecue-roasted Chicken until thermometer registers 185° F or until meat near thighbone is no longer pink when slashed (4 to 4½ hours; allow about 12 minutes per pound). Several times during cooking, place a rosemary sprig on coals; during last hour, brush turkey with remaining port several times.

Discard stuffing and transfer turkey to a warm platter or board. Makes 16 servings. *Calories per serving: 215.*

GRILLED GAME HENS WITH JALAPEÑO JELLY GLAZE

(Pictured on page 78)

Preparation time: 5 to 10 minutes
Grilling time: 30 to 40 minutes

Calories per serving: 338

3 **Rock Cornish game hens (1½ lbs. *each*), thawed if frozen**

1 **tablespoon butter or margarine**

¼ **cup jalapeño jelly**

2 **teaspoons lime juice**

Basted with a sweet-hot jalapeño glaze, plump game hens sizzle to juicy perfection on the grill.

Using poultry scissors, cut each game hen in half through backbone and breastbone. Remove giblets and reserve for other uses. Rinse hens and pat dry.

In a small pan, combine butter and jelly; stir over medium-high heat until melted. Remove from heat and stir in lime juice.

Place hen halves, skin side up, on a barbecue grill 4 to 6 inches above a solid bed of medium-hot coals. Grill, turning several times and basting with jelly mixture during last 15 minutes, until hens are browned and breast meat in thickest portion is no longer pink when slashed (30 to 40 minutes). Makes 6 servings.

Per serving: 43 grams protein, 9 grams carbohydrates, 13 grams total fat, 10 grams unsaturated fat, 202 milligrams cholesterol, 26 milligrams sodium.

GROUND TURKEY SAUCE WITH SPAGHETTI SQUASH

Preparation time: 10 to 15 minutes
Cooking time: 1¼ to 1½ hours

Calories per serving: 389

1 **medium-size spaghetti squash (1½ to 2 lbs.)**

1 **pound ground turkey**

1 **large onion, finely chopped**

2 **cloves garlic, minced or pressed**

6 **ounces mushrooms, thinly sliced**

1 **medium-size carrot, finely chopped**

1 **large can (16 oz.) tomato sauce**

1 **small can (8 oz.) tomato sauce**

1½ **teaspoons oregano leaves**

1 **teaspoon dry basil**

½ **teaspoon *each* sugar and salt**

¼ **teaspoon pepper**

1 **bay leaf**

¼ **cup grated Parmesan cheese**

Here's a lighthearted—and light—version of spaghetti that features a ground turkey sauce served on a bed of tender spaghettilike strands of squash. The squash can be baked or microwaved.

Pierce squash in several places with a fork. Place on a rimmed baking sheet. Bake, uncovered, in a 350° oven, turning after 45 minutes, until shell gives when pressed (1¼ to 1½ hours *total*).

About 45 minutes before squash is done, crumble ground turkey into a wide nonstick frying pan over medium heat, breaking up large pieces with a spoon. Add onion, garlic, mushrooms, and carrot. Cook, stirring often, until most of the liquid has evaporated.

Stir in all tomato sauce, oregano, basil, sugar, salt, pepper, and bay leaf; cover and simmer for 30 minutes. Uncover and boil gently, stirring occasionally, until thickened.

Cut squash in half; scrape out and discard seeds. Loosen squash strands and scoop out into a warm serving bowl, mounding squash around edge of bowl. Spoon turkey sauce into center. Offer cheese to sprinkle over individual portions. Makes 4 servings.

Note: To microwave squash, cut in half lengthwise; scrape out and discard seeds. Place squash, hollow side up, in a 9- by 13-inch microwave-safe baking dish. Cover with plastic wrap. Microwave on **HIGH (100%)** for 12 to 14 minutes, rotating each piece a half-turn after 5 minutes, or until squash is fork-tender. Let stand, covered, for 5 minutes.

Per serving: 28 grams protein, 38 grams carbohydrates, 17 grams total fat, .47 gram unsaturated fat, 5 milligrams cholesterol, 1465 milligrams sodium.

TURKEY SCALOPPINE WITH PEPPERS

(Pictured on facing page)

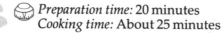

Preparation time: 20 minutes
Cooking time: About 25 minutes

Calories per serving: 306

- 1 **pound boneless turkey breast, cut into ¼-inch-thick slices**
- 2 **tablespoons all-purpose flour**
- 2 **tablespoons butter or margarine**
- 3 **medium-size red or yellow bell peppers (about 1 lb. *total*), seeded and cut into ¼-inch strips**
- 1 **tablespoon salad oil**
- ⅓ **cup shredded Swiss or fontina cheese**
- **Freshly ground pepper**
- **Lemon wedges**

Red bell peppers and a touch of melted cheese dress up tender, delicate turkey breast cooked in the style of veal scaloppine.

Place turkey slices, one at a time, between 2 pieces of plastic wrap or wax paper and pound with a flat-surfaced mallet until ⅛ inch thick. (At this point, you may lay pounded slices slightly apart in single layers between pieces of wax paper or plastic wrap; cover and refrigerate for up to 2 days.)

Coat turkey slices lightly with flour, shaking off excess.

In a wide nonstick frying pan, melt 1 tablespoon of the butter over medium heat. Add bell peppers and cook, stirring, until limp (10 to 12 minutes). Remove from pan with a slotted spoon.

To pan add oil and remaining 1 tablespoon butter. Increase heat to medium-high. Add turkey pieces, a few at a time (do not crowd pan), and cook, turning once, until lightly browned on both sides (1½ to 2 minutes *total*). As turkey is cooked, transfer pieces to an ovenproof serving platter, overlapping slightly. When all turkey is cooked, spoon bell peppers over and around turkey. Sprinkle evenly with cheese.

Bake in a 400° oven just until cheese is melted (3 to 5 minutes). Sprinkle with ground pepper. Serve with lemon wedges. Makes 4 servings.

Per serving: 34 grams protein, 11 grams carbohydrates, 17 grams total fat, 6 grams unsaturated fat, 29 milligrams cholesterol, 165 milligrams sodium.

Turkey Scaloppine with Mushrooms

Follow directions for Turkey Scaloppine with Peppers, but omit bell peppers, cheese, and ground pepper.

In a wide nonstick frying pan, melt 1 tablespoon of the butter with oil over medium-high heat. Prepare and cook turkey as described at left, transferring cooked pieces to a warm platter; keep warm.

When all turkey is cooked, add remaining 1 tablespoon butter to pan with ½ pound medium-size **mushrooms.** Cook, stirring often, until mushrooms are slightly browned. Add ½ cup **marsala** or sherry, scraping pan to free brown bits. With a slotted spoon, transfer mushrooms to platter with turkey.

Bring liquid in pan to a boil over high heat. Cook, stirring, until slightly reduced and syrupy. Pour over turkey. Garnish with lemon wedges and **parsley sprigs.** Makes 4 servings (248 calories per serving).

BARBECUED TURKEY BREAST STEAKS

Preparation time: 5 minutes
Grilling time: 5 to 8 minutes

Calories per serving: 259

- 1½ **pounds boneless turkey breast, cut into ½- to ¾-inch-thick slices**
- 2 **tablespoons olive oil or salad oil**
- ¼ **teaspoon salt**
- **Seasoned pepper**
- **Fresh cilantro sprigs**

For an unusual low-calorie touch, accompany these simple grilled turkey breast slices with one of the fresh, piquant salsas on page 92.

Brush turkey breast slices all over with oil. Place turkey slices on a barbecue grill 4 to 6 inches above a bed of hot coals. Grill, turning once, until

slices are lightly browned and meat in center is no longer pink when slashed (5 to 8 minutes *total*). Sprinkle with salt and pepper and garnish with cilantro. Makes 4 servings.

Per serving: 44 grams protein, 0 grams carbohydrates, 13 grams total fat, 5 grams unsaturated fat, 119 milligrams cholesterol, 133 milligrams sodium.

A little skillet magic transforms lean turkey
into an elegant classic. To conjure up Turkey Scaloppine with Peppers
(facing page), you sauté red bell peppers and pounded turkey breast, melt
a touch of Swiss cheese over all, and voilà—scaloppine!

L·E·A·N & T·R·I·M

Meat, one of nature's best sources of complete protein and iron, is also one of the good cook's best sources of inspiration for delicious dishes of all kinds. Beef, lamb, and pork appear in every kind of preparation, from easy grills to elegant sautés to tantalizing ethnic dishes.

Variety and moderation, two hallmarks of light cuisine, are especially applicable when you're thinking about meat. Eating meat and eating light can be perfectly compatible: what's essential is to select leaner cuts, prepare them in varied ways, and serve them up in moderate portions.

Versatile meat. As you'll see from the recipes in this chapter, there's no shortage of ways to cook meat to juicy perfection. From the grill, we feature a variety of recipes—from simple Pounded Lamb Chops with Rosemary (page 96) to Fajitas (page 87), a lively offering from Mexico that combines marinated flank steak and onions with a spirited salsa for an unusual burrito. From the oven comes a simple favorite—Oven-barbecued Beef Burgers (page 89), a flavorful and lean ground beef dish. And from the frying pan or wok, we offer sautés and stir-fries, from stylish Veal Sauté with Peas (page 95) to succulent stir-fried Mongolian Lamb with Spring Onions (page 97).

Go for the lean. Selecting meats for light cooking means looking for the leaner cuts. When you shop for beef, choose round rather than loin cuts. Boneless top round (it's in our Beef & Vegetable Sauté on the facing page) chalks up 894 calories per pound, as compared with 1725 for the same amount of boneless club steak.

Whether it's spicy with hot seasonings or aromatic with herbs and wine, meat makes a satisfying main dish that's packed with good, healthy protein. And if you buy it lean, cook it to perfection, and serve it in moderate portions, you'll find that eating meat can be part of eating light!

Similarly, pork cuts can vary greatly in fat content. Bone-in loin chops, like those in lively Grilled Gingered Pork Chops (page 98), have 1065 calories per pound, versus an average of 1220 calories for chops from the fattier shoulder.

Lamb from the leg (we've called for it in Mongolian Lamb with Spring Onions on page 97) adds up to 845 calories per pound; in contrast, rib lamb chops have 1229 calories.

Ground meats often contain more fat than you may want. Of course, some fat is desirable because it keeps the meat from drying out as it cooks. But as with other cuts of meat, it's smart to look for the leaner mixtures.

About the leanest ground beef you can find is 18 percent fat. Generally, ground lamb, veal, and pork are not marked with their fat content. You may be able to get the information at your meat counter, or you can buy a cut you know is lean, then trim and grind it at home.

Trimming and skimming. To lighten the calorie load of the meat you buy, carefully trim the fat from the meat before you cook it. Cut off any remaining fat as you eat. The calorie totals for our recipes reflect the composition of typical cuts of meat as usually trimmed for sale; if you cut away fat conscientiously, you can lower these amounts.

We also recommend pouring off and discarding drippings after you brown meat. And when you cook a meaty soup or stew, allow time for it to cool in the refrigerator. This way, you can remove the layer of excess fat on the surface before reheating.

M·E·A·T·S

SWEET-SOUR FLANK STEAK

Preparation time: 10 minutes
Marinating time: 4 hours or more
Grilling time: 8 to 10 minutes

Calories per serving: 217

⅓ cup cider vinegar

¼ cup *each* honey and soy sauce

1 clove garlic, minced or pressed

⅛ teaspoon liquid hot pepper seasoning

1 flank steak (about 1½ lbs.)

Vegetable oil cooking spray

Parsley sprigs

Light and lean flank steak comes off the grill juicy and full of flavor when it's marinated, then cooked just to the rare stage.

In a small pan, combine vinegar, honey, soy sauce, garlic, and hot pepper seasoning. Place over medium heat and cook, stirring often, until honey is dissolved and mixture is well blended (about 5 minutes). Let cool slightly.

Trim and discard any fat from meat; place steak in a shallow bowl or baking dish. Pour vinegar mixture over steak, cover, and refrigerate for at least 4 hours or until next day, turning steak once or twice.

Remove steak from marinade and drain briefly, reserving marinade. Spray a barbecue grill with cooking spray. Place steak on grill 4 to 6 inches above a solid bed of medium coals. Grill, turning once and basting often with some of the marinade, until done to your liking when slashed (about 4 minutes on each side for rare).

Transfer steak to a carving board and keep warm. In a small pan, boil any remaining marinade over high heat until reduced to about ½ cup. Cut meat across grain into thin, slanting slices. Garnish with parsley. Accompany with marinade. Makes 6 servings.

Per serving: 25 grams protein, 14 grams carbohydrates, 7 grams total fat, 3 grams unsaturated fat, 77 milligrams cholesterol, 972 milligrams sodium.

BEEF & VEGETABLE SAUTÉ

Preparation time: 12 to 15 minutes
Cooking time: 15 to 20 minutes

Calories per serving: 351

⅓ cup firmly packed brown sugar

2 tablespoons cornstarch

¼ cup cider vinegar

3 tablespoons soy sauce

1½ pounds top round or flank steak (½ to ¾ inch thick)

2 tablespoons butter or margarine

1 large onion, thinly sliced

1½ cups thinly sliced carrots

1 cup green beans, cut into 1-inch lengths

1 cup water

1½ cups thinly sliced zucchini

Cook this colorful dish in a flash, the Asian way. You stir-fry lean beef first, then toss a bright mix of vegetables into the pan. It all gets stirred together with a flavorful, slightly sweet sauce.

In a small bowl, combine brown sugar, cornstarch, vinegar, and soy sauce; stir until cornstarch is dissolved. Set aside.

Trim and discard any fat from meat. Cut meat into slanting slices ⅛ to ¼ inch thick.

In a wide nonstick frying pan, melt 1 tablespoon of the butter over medium-high heat. Add meat strips, a few at a time, and cook, stirring, until well browned, adding remaining 1 tablespoon butter as needed; lift out meat as it browns and set aside.

When all meat is cooked, add onion, carrots, beans, and ½ cup of the water to pan; stir well, cover, and cook, stirring often, for 8 minutes. Stir in zucchini and remaining ½ cup water; cook, uncovered, just until vegetables are tender to bite (about 2 more minutes).

Stir cornstarch mixture and add to vegetables along with meat; cook, stirring, until sauce boils and thickens. Serve immediately. Makes 6 servings.

Per serving: 25 grams protein, 23 grams carbohydrates, 18 grams total fat, 8 grams unsaturated fat, 89 milligrams cholesterol, 805 milligrams sodium.

Here's a light salad with a difference!
Give lean, marinated sirloin strips a speedy stir-fry, then
combine them with cool watercress and onions to create Hot Beef & Watercress
Salad (facing page). Fresh tangerines make a refreshing dessert.

HOT BEEF & WATERCRESS SALAD
(Pictured on facing page)

Preparation time: 20 minutes
Marinating time: 30 minutes or more
Cooking time: About 3 minutes

Calories per serving: 427

½ **pound lean boneless beef steak, such as top sirloin (about 1 inch thick), fat removed**
4 **cloves garlic, minced or pressed**
2 **teaspoons soy sauce**
1 **teaspoon sugar**
3 **teaspoons salad oil**
2 **tablespoons white wine vinegar**
¼ **teaspoon pepper**
1 **small white onion, thinly sliced**
About ½ pound watercress

For this unusual hot and cold main-dish salad, you place stir-fried beef strips on a bed of cool watercress.

Cut steak into ⅛-inch-thick slices, about 3 inches long. In a medium-size bowl, mix beef, garlic, soy sauce, ½ teaspoon of the sugar, and 1 teaspoon of the oil. Cover and refrigerate for at least 30 minutes or until next day.

In another bowl, stir together remaining ½ teaspoon sugar, remaining 2 teaspoons oil, vinegar, and pepper. Add onion (separate into rings) and mix lightly. Cover and refrigerate for at least 30 minutes or until next day.

Remove and discard tough watercress stems. Measure 3 cups sprigs, lightly packed. Shortly before serving, add watercress to onion mixture, mixing lightly to coat. Arrange on 2 dinner plates.

Place a wide nonstick frying pan or wok over high heat until pan is hot. Add beef mixture and stir-fry until beef is lightly browned (about 2 minutes). Arrange steak strips on watercress salads. Makes 2 servings.

Per serving: 25 grams protein, 10 grams carbohydrates, 21 grams total fat, 12 grams unsaturated fat, 77 milligrams cholesterol, 548 milligrams sodium.

FAJITAS

Preparation time: 30 minutes
Marinating time: 4 hours or more
Grilling time: About 20 minutes

Calories per serving: 475

2 **pounds flank steak**
⅓ **cup lime juice**
¼ **cup salad oil or olive oil**
¼ **cup tequila or additional lime juice**
3 **cloves garlic, minced or pressed**
1 **teaspoon ground cumin**
¾ **teaspoon oregano leaves**
¼ **teaspoon pepper**
3 **small onions (unpeeled), cut in half lengthwise**
Salsa Fresca (recipe follows)
6 **green onions (with roots attached)**
Vegetable oil cooking spray
6 **flour tortillas (8 inches in diameter)**
1 **cup plain yogurt**
Fresh cilantro (coriander) sprigs

From Mexico come fajitas (fah-HEE-tahs), burritos filled with lime-marinated steak and grilled onions.

Trim and discard any fat from steak. Place in a 9- by 13-inch baking dish. In a small bowl, mix lime juice, oil, tequila, garlic, cumin, oregano, and pepper; pour over meat, turning to coat. Place onion halves, cut side down, in marinade. Cover and refrigerate for at least 4 hours or until next day, turning meat several times.

Meanwhile, prepare Salsa Fresca.

With a string, tie green onions together about 3 inches from roots to form a brush.

Spray a barbecue grill with cooking spray. Place onion halves on grill 4 to 6 inches above a solid bed of medium coals. Grill for about 7 minutes, then turn. Remove meat from marinade and drain briefly, reserving marinade. Place meat on grill. Baste meat and onion halves with marinade, using green onion brush.

Grill onion halves until soft (6 to 8 more minutes). Grill beef, turning once, until done to your liking when slashed (3 to 5 minutes on each side for rare). Transfer meat and onions to a board; keep warm.

Roll green onion brush in marinade; then grill, turning often, until wilted (3 to 5 minutes). Place on board and untie. Cut meat across grain into thin, slanting slices.

Heat tortillas on grill, turning often, just until soft (15 to 30 seconds).

Place a few meat slices down center of each tortilla. Top with some onion pieces, salsa, yogurt, and cilantro. Fold up to enclose. Accompany with green onions. Makes 6 servings.

Salsa Fresca. Prepare a triple recipe of **Fresh Tomato Salsa** (page 92), substituting **lime juice** for oil.

Per serving: 38 grams protein, 29 grams carbohydrates, 20 grams total fat, 12 grams unsaturated fat, 106 milligrams cholesterol, 232 milligrams sodium.

BURGUNDY BEEF

Preparation time: 10 minutes
Marinating time: 15 minutes or more
Cooking time: 6 to 8 minutes

Calories per serving: 420

1	pound lean boneless beef steak, such as top sirloin (about ¾ inch thick)
¼	pound mushrooms
½	cup dry red wine
1½	tablespoons butter or margarine
¼	teaspoon *each* dry chervil, dry tarragon, and salt
⅛	teaspoon marjoram leaves
1½	tablespoons all-purpose flour

Red wine and savory herbs go into an aromatic marinade and sauce for this light but hearty beef dish.

Trim and discard fat from meat. Cut steak into ⅛-inch-thick slices, 2 to 3 inches long. Thinly slice mushrooms. In a medium-size bowl, combine beef and mushrooms. Cover with wine. Let stand at room temperature for about 15 minutes or cover and refrigerate for up to 3 hours.

Lift meat and mushrooms from marinade and drain, reserving marinade. In a wide nonstick frying pan, melt butter over medium heat; stir in chervil, tarragon, salt, and marjoram. Add meat and mushrooms. Cook, stirring, just until meat is no longer pink (4 to 5 minutes).

Sprinkle with flour, blend in marinade, and cook, stirring, until slightly thickened. Makes 4 servings.

Per serving: 20 grams protein, 5 grams carbohydrates, 35 grams total fat, 15 grams unsaturated fat, 91 milligrams cholesterol, 259 milligrams sodium.

LIGHT TOUCHES: THE LIGHT APPROACH TO WINE

A splash of sherry to enliven a quick lamb sauté, a ruby-hued red wine marinade to flavor flank steak—is wine compatible with light cuisine?

The alcohol in wine, the source of most of the calories, evaporates when you heat to 172°F (but not necessarily boil) a mixture made with wine. Left behind are only the wine's flavor and aroma—and less than 20 percent of its original calories.

If you drink wine with your meal, figure on about 100 calories for 4 ounces of dry red or white wine.

GROUND BEEF PATTIES WITH LEMON SAUCE

Preparation time: 10 minutes
Cooking time: 15 to 20 minutes

Calories per serving: 360

1	egg
1	teaspoon grated lemon peel
½	teaspoon salt
2	tablespoons finely chopped onion
1½	pounds lean ground beef
1	tablespoon salad oil
2	tablespoons white wine vinegar
½	teaspoon ground ginger
3	tablespoons firmly packed brown sugar
1	bay leaf
6	thin lemon slices
1	beef bouillon cube

To make this speedy main dish, brown meat patties, then simmer them briefly in a lemony tart-sweet sauce.

In a large bowl, beat egg, lemon peel, and salt. Add onion and ground beef, mixing lightly until well combined. Shape meat mixture into 6 thick patties of equal size.

Heat oil in a wide nonstick frying pan over medium-high heat. Add patties and cook, turning once, until well browned on both sides. Remove from pan and set aside. Pour out and discard any fat in pan.

To pan add vinegar, ginger, brown sugar, bay leaf, lemon slices, and bouillon cube. Bring mixture to a boil.

Return patties to pan; reduce heat, cover, and simmer until meat is done to your liking when slashed (about 8 minutes for medium-well). Remove and discard bay leaf. To serve, spoon sauce over patties. Makes 6 servings.

Per serving: 25 grams protein, 6 grams carbohydrates, 15 grams total fat, 8 grams unsaturated fat, 120 milligrams cholesterol, 432 milligrams sodium.

OVEN-BARBECUED BEEF BURGERS

Preparation time: 10 minutes
Baking time: 40 to 50 minutes

Calories per serving: 393

½ cup nonfat milk

1 egg

1 cup soft French bread crumbs

½ teaspoon *each* salt and oregano leaves

1 small onion, cut into quarters

1½ pounds lean ground beef

Vegetable oil cooking spray

⅔ cup catsup

2 tablespoons red wine vinegar

1 tablespoon *each* brown sugar, Worcestershire, and Dijon mustard

Serve it as a meat loaf, or sandwich it between split, toasted French rolls. Either way, this oven-baked beef dish, with its glaze of sweet-tangy barbecue sauce, is sure to satisfy the heartiest appetites.

In a blender or food processor, combine milk, egg, bread crumbs, salt, oregano, and onion; whirl until puréed. Add to beef in a large bowl, mixing lightly.

Spray a 9-inch-square baking pan with cooking spray. Pat meat mixture evenly into pan. (At this point, you may cover and refrigerate until next day.)

Bake, uncovered, in a 375° oven for 30 minutes (40 minutes if refrigerated). Meanwhile, combine catsup, vinegar, brown sugar, Worcestershire, and mustard in a small pan; bring to a boil over medium-high heat, stirring until sugar is dissolved. Spoon over meat. Bake for 10 more minutes. Makes 6 servings.

Per serving: 27 grams protein, 16 grams carbohydrates, 13 grams total fat, 6 grams unsaturated fat, 120 milligrams cholesterol, 699 milligrams sodium.

LETTUCE TACOS

Preparation time: 25 minutes
Cooking time: 8 to 10 minutes

Calories per serving: 479

2 medium-size carrots

1 large zucchini (7 to 8 inches long)

1 tablespoon salad oil

1 cup corn cut from cob or frozen corn

1 pound lean ground beef

2 cloves garlic, minced or pressed

1 tablespoon chili powder

1 teaspoon ground cumin

1 cup thinly sliced green onions (including tops)

1 can (6 oz.) spicy tomato cocktail

1 tablespoon cornstarch

¼ teaspoon salt

½ cup shredded jack cheese

1 medium-size head iceberg lettuce (about 1 lb.)

Spoon this spicy meat-and-vegetable mixture into cool, crisp lettuce leaves for an informal main dish that's much lighter than the usual tortilla-wrapped tacos. For an even spicier version, add bottled hot chile salsa to taste.

Coarsely chop carrots. Cut zucchini into ¼-inch cubes.

Place a wide nonstick frying pan or wok over high heat. When pan is hot, add oil and carrots; stir-fry for 1 minute. Add zucchini and corn; stir-fry for 1 more minute, then remove vegetables with a slotted spoon and set aside.

Crumble beef into pan; cook, stirring, until browned (2 to 3 minutes). Spoon off and discard all but 1 tablespoon of the fat. Add garlic, chili powder, cumin, and onions; cook, stirring, just until onions begin to soften. Return carrot mixture to pan and cook, stirring, until heated through.

Mix tomato cocktail and cornstarch; add to pan and cook, stirring, until sauce boils and thickens. Add salt. Transfer to a serving bowl; sprinkle with cheese. Separate leaves from head of lettuce.

To serve, spoon beef mixture onto lettuce leaves. Makes 4 servings.

Per serving: 30 grams protein, 25 grams carbohydrates, 19 grams total fat, 9 grams unsaturated fat, 86 milligrams cholesterol, 411 milligrams sodium.

CHILES RELLENOS MEATBALLS
(Pictured on facing page)

Preparation time: About 20 minutes
Baking time: About 40 minutes

Calories per serving: 438

1	egg
¼	cup nonfat milk
⅓	cup fine dry bread crumbs
1	tablespoon chopped parsley
1	pound lean ground beef
1	can (4 oz.) whole green chiles
10	pimento-stuffed green olives
	Tomato-Chile Sauce (recipe follows)
¼	cup shredded jack cheese

Chiles in the meatballs, chiles in the sauce—this lively dish delivers hearty Mexican flavor.

In a large bowl, beat egg and milk until blended. Mix in bread crumbs and parsley. Add ground beef, mixing lightly until well combined. Divide meat mixture into 10 equal portions.

Cut chiles lengthwise into ten 1-inch-wide strips; reserve remaining chiles for sauce. Wrap a chile strip around each olive. Carefully mold a portion of meat around each chile-wrapped olive.

Place stuffed meatballs in a shallow 10- by 15-inch baking pan. Bake, uncovered, in a 450° oven until browned (about 20 minutes).

Meanwhile, prepare Tomato-Chile Sauce.

Transfer meatballs to a shallow 2-quart casserole, discarding drippings from baking pan. Spoon tomato sauce over and around meatballs. Sprinkle with cheese. Reduce oven temperature to 350° and bake, uncovered, until heated through (about 20 minutes). Makes 4 servings.

Tomato-Chile Sauce. In a 2- to 3-quart pan, combine ½ cup chopped **onion**, 1 clove **garlic**, minced or pressed, 1 can (1 lb.) ready-cut **tomatoes**, ¾ teaspoon **oregano leaves**, ⅛ teaspoon **ground cumin**, and reserved **green chiles**, chopped. Bring to a gentle boil over medium heat and cook, uncovered, stirring often, until reduced to 2 cups.

Per serving: 30 grams protein, 16 grams carbohydrates, 17 grams total fat, 8 grams unsaturated fat, 147 milligrams cholesterol, 593 milligrams sodium.

GROUND BEEF PIZZA

Preparation time: 20 minutes
Baking time: About 25 minutes

Calories per serving: 409

1	egg
2	tablespoons *each* fine dry bread crumbs and finely chopped onion
½	teaspoon salt
¼	teaspoon pepper
1	teaspoon Italian herb seasoning or ¼ teaspoon *each* dry basil, marjoram, oregano, and thyme leaves
1	pound lean ground beef
2	medium-size tomatoes
1	green bell pepper
½	cup shredded jack or Cheddar cheese
1	teaspoon oregano leaves

Here's a switch—in this pizza, ground beef forms the crust! It cradles a filling of herbed, cheese-sprinkled vegetables.

In a large bowl, beat egg until blended. Mix in bread crumbs, onion, ¼ teaspoon of the salt, pepper, and herb seasoning. Add ground beef, mixing lightly until well combined. Lightly press meat mixture over bottom and sides of a 9-inch pie pan.

Peel and slice tomatoes. Cutting from stem end, core and seed bell pepper, then slice crosswise into ¼-inch-thick rings. Arrange tomato slices and bell pepper rings over meat; sprinkle with remaining ¼ teaspoon salt, cheese, and oregano.

Bake, uncovered, in a 400° oven until meat is cooked through (about 25 minutes). To serve, cut into wedges. Makes 4 servings.

Per serving: 30 grams protein, 6 grams carbohydrates, 18 grams total fat, 8 grams unsaturated fat, 154 milligrams cholesterol, 490 milligrams sodium.

Eating light doesn't mean doing away with hearty,
stick-to-the-ribs dishes—not when you cook spicy Chiles
Rellenos Meatballs (facing page). Topped with robust chile-tomato sauce
and a sprinkling of jack cheese, they're deceptively easy on the calories.

Carrot & Sweet Pepper Salsa

Enliven raw oysters or steamed clams with this brightly colored salsa.

- 2 **medium-size carrots**
- 1 **medium-size green, red, or yellow bell pepper**
- ½ **cup minced shallots or red onion**
- 6 **tablespoons white wine vinegar**
- 2 **tablespoons firmly packed brown sugar**
- 1 **tablespoon minced fresh ginger**
- 2 **large cloves garlic, minced or pressed**
  Salt (optional)

Shred carrots. Seed and dice bell pepper. In a medium-size bowl, combine carrots, bell pepper, shallots, vinegar, brown sugar, ginger, and garlic; stir until sugar is dissolved. Season with salt to taste, if desired.

Cover and refrigerate for at least 1 hour or for up to 2 days. Serve cold. Makes about 3 cups. *Calories per serving (1 tablespoon):* 4.

SLIMMING SAUCES

Nothing lifts a simple dish out of the ordinary like a wonderful sauce. Now you can create sauces that add zest and sparkle to food without extra calories. Do it the Latin American way, with a fresh, zippy salsa made from vegetables or fruits. Or whip up a creamy lemon-garlic sauce for your vegetables.

Fresh Tomato Salsa

Spoon this piquant salsa over meats, poultry, even salads. At only 12 calories per tablespoon, why not?

- 1 **small fresh hot green chile (serrano or jalapeño), seeded and finely chopped**
- 1 **tablespoon chopped fresh cilantro (coriander)**
- 4 **green onions (including tops), thinly sliced**
- 1 **large tomato, peeled, seeded, and finely chopped**
- 1 **tablespoon olive oil or salad oil**
- 1 **tablespoon red wine vinegar**

In a medium-size bowl, combine chile, cilantro, onions, tomato, oil, and vinegar. Mix lightly until evenly blended.

If made ahead, cover and refrigerate until next day. Stir well just before serving. Makes about 1 cup. *Calories per serving (1 tablespoon):* 12.

Roasted Salsa

Charring the tomatoes and chiles for this salsa gives it an intriguing smoky flavor that enhances pork or beef ribs. Serve the salsa hot or make it ahead and offer it at room temperature.

- 3 **large ripe tomatoes**
- 4 **large fresh mild green or red chiles, such as Anaheim, pasilla, or poblano**
- 2 **tablespoons *each* red wine vinegar and chopped fresh cilantro (coriander)**
- 2 **cloves garlic, minced or pressed**
- ¼ **teaspoon salt**

Place tomatoes on a barbecue grill 4 to 6 inches above a solid bed of hot coals. Grill, turning tomatoes as skins split, for 5 minutes.

Add chiles to grill with tomatoes. Grill vegetables, turning as needed, until chile skins are charred on all sides and tomatoes are hot (7 to 10 minutes for chiles and about 10 more minutes for tomatoes). Remove and discard chile stems.

On a board, coarsely chop tomatoes and chiles. In a medium-size bowl, combine chopped vegetables and their juices, vinegar, cilantro, garlic, and salt. Stir until blended. Serve hot or at room temperature.

If made ahead, let stand at room temperature for up to 4 hours, or cover and refrigerate until next day. Makes about 2½ cups. *Calories per serving (1 tablespoon):* 4.

Cucumber & Mixed Herb Salsa

Here's a refreshing complement to grilled fish, meat, or poultry; or try it with cold poached salmon.

½ cup white wine vinegar

¼ cup *each* minced fresh cilantro (coriander) and minced fresh mint leaves

2 tablespoons minced fresh dill or 2 teaspoons dill weed

4 teaspoons Dijon mustard

2 teaspoons sugar

2 large cucumbers, peeled, seeded, and diced

1 large firm-ripe tomato, cored, seeded, and diced

¼ teaspoon salt

In a medium-size bowl, stir together vinegar, cilantro, mint, dill, mustard, and sugar. Mix in cucumbers, tomato, and salt. Cover and refrigerate for at least 1 hour or for up to 2 days. Serve cold. Makes 3½ cups. *Calories per serving (1 tablespoon): 3.*

Tropical Fruit Salsa

This delectable fruit mélange adds something special to stews, as well as to grilled teriyaki beef or chicken.

1 medium-size firm-ripe mango

1 cup *each* diced fresh pineapple and diced honeydew melon

½ cup diced red bell pepper

⅓ cup seasoned rice wine vinegar; or ⅓ cup rice wine vinegar mixed with 1 tablespoon sugar and salt to taste

2 tablespoons minced fresh cilantro (coriander)

½ teaspoon crushed red pepper

2 large kiwi fruit

Peel mango and cut fruit off pit in about ½-inch cubes; discard pit. In a medium-size bowl, mix mango, pineapple, melon, bell pepper, vinegar, cilantro, and red pepper. (At this point, you may cover and refrigerate for up to 2 days.)

Just before serving, peel kiwi and cut into about ¼-inch cubes; add to salsa mixture. Makes about 4 cups. *Calories per serving (1 tablespoon): 7.*

Lemon-Garlic Cream Sauce

Dress up hot artichokes, asparagus, or broccoli with this light version of a classic mousseline sauce.

¼ cup *each* dry white wine and water

1 chicken bouillon cube

½ cup whipping cream

2 tablespoons butter or margarine

1 small clove garlic, minced or pressed

2 tablespoons all-purpose flour

1 large egg yolk

2 tablespoons lemon juice

Pour wine and water into a small bowl. Crumble bouillon cube into mixture; set aside.

In a medium-size bowl, whip cream until soft peaks form; set aside.

In a small pan, melt butter over low heat. Add garlic and cook until softened but not browned. With a wire whisk, stir in flour, cooking until bubbly (do not brown). Remove from heat and gradually add wine mixture, stirring until smooth. Cook over medium heat, stirring, until sauce comes to a boil.

Remove from heat and whisk in egg yolk and lemon juice. Fold into whipped cream; serve hot. If made ahead, set bowl in hot water to keep sauce warm for up to 3 hours. Makes about 1½ cups. *Calories per serving (1 tablespoon): 33.*

Red pepper, lemon juice, fresh oranges, cumin, and
mustard seeds combine to make stylish Veal Sauté with Peas
(facing page), a dish for the truly adventurous. Peas, rice, and a simple green
onion garnish are perfect foils for the complex flavors of the veal.

VEAL SAUTÉ WITH PEAS
(Pictured on facing page)

Preparation time: 15 minutes
Cooking time: 12 to 15 minutes

Calories per serving: 362

---

1 **pound boneless veal round (about ¼ inch thick)**

1 **teaspoon mustard seeds**

½ **teaspoon crushed red pepper**

⅛ **teaspoon cumin seeds**

2 **tablespoons all-purpose flour**

2 **tablespoons butter or margarine**

1 **tablespoon salad oil**

1 **package (10 oz.) frozen peas, thawed**

3 **tablespoons orange-flavored liqueur or orange juice**

1 **tablespoon lemon juice**

2 **teaspoons soy sauce**

1 **medium-size orange, peeled and thinly sliced**

2 **green onions (including tops), cut in half lengthwise**

A sauté for sophisticated tastes, this dish features boneless veal boldly seasoned with mustard seeds, red pepper, and cumin, then topped with an orange- and lemon-flavored sauce.

Trim and discard any tough membrane and fat from veal; cut into serving-size pieces. Place, well apart, on a large piece of plastic wrap. In a small bowl, combine mustard seeds, red pepper, and cumin seeds; sprinkle mixture evenly over top of veal. Cover with more plastic wrap; pound with a flat-surfaced mallet until about ⅛ inch thick. Coat lightly with flour on all sides.

In a wide nonstick frying pan, melt 1 tablespoon of the butter with oil over medium-high heat. When butter begins to brown, add veal pieces, a few at a time (do not crowd pan), and cook, turning once, until browned on both sides (2 to 4 minutes *total*). As veal is browned, remove from pan and arrange in a single layer in a shallow rimmed baking pan. When all

veal is cooked, set frying pan aside, reserving drippings.

Pour peas into a 9-inch-square baking pan. Place peas and veal, uncovered, in a 450° oven until heated through (about 5 minutes). Meanwhile, add remaining 1 tablespoon butter to frying pan along with liqueur, lemon juice, and soy sauce. Place over medium-high heat and cook, stirring well to combine with pan drippings, until sauce boils. Remove from heat briefly.

Arrange veal slices on a serving platter or dinner plates, overlapping pieces; pour any accumulated pan juices from veal into sauce. Tuck orange slices between veal pieces; spoon peas alongside. Quickly bring sauce to a boil again and spoon over veal. Garnish with onions. Makes 4 servings.

Per serving: 27 grams protein, 18 grams carbohydrates, 20 grams total fat, 10 grams unsaturated fat, 99 milligrams cholesterol, 458 milligrams sodium.

GRILLED VEAL CHOPS WITH LEMON & THYME

Preparation time: 10 minutes
Grilling time: 4 to 5 minutes

Calories per serving: 289

---

3 **tablespoons minced fresh thyme leaves or 1½ tablespoons dry thyme leaves**

2 **teaspoons grated lemon peel**

½ **cup finely chopped parsley**

2 **tablespoons olive oil or salad oil**

4 **veal rib or loin chops (¾ to 1 inch thick; about 1¼ lbs. *total*)**

Vegetable oil cooking spray

Lemon wedges

Lemon, parsley, and thyme impart appealing flavor to these veal chops; pounding the chops before cooking helps work the mixture into the meat and reduces the grilling time. Leave the bone on the side of each chop attached.

In a small bowl, mix thyme, lemon peel, parsley, and oil. Slash connective tissue around each veal chop at about 1-inch intervals. Rub about 1½ teaspoons of the thyme mixture on each side of each chop.

Place 1 or 2 chops between large pieces of plastic wrap. With a flat-surfaced mallet, pound meat evenly and firmly until about ¼ inch thick.

(At this point, you may cover and refrigerate for up to 8 hours.)

Spray a barbecue grill with cooking spray. Place chops on grill 4 to 6 inches above a solid bed of hot coals. Grill, turning once, until done to your liking when slashed (4 to 5 minutes *total* for medium). Garnish with lemon wedges. Makes 4 servings.

Per serving: 21 grams protein, .79 gram carbohydrates, 22 grams total fat, 13 grams unsaturated fat, 78 milligrams cholesterol, 75 milligrams sodium.

MUSTARD-GLAZED VEAL STRIPS

Preparation time: 30 minutes
Baking time: About 1¼ hours

Calories per serving: 444

2	**pounds boneless veal stew meat**
2	**tablespoons salad oil**
	Mustard Sauce (recipe follows)
¾	**pound watercress**
1	**medium-size ripe avocado**
1	**large ripe papaya**
2	**tablespoons lemon juice**
	Lemon wedges

For a delectable make-ahead dish for company, try lightly sauced veal accompanied by avocado, papaya, and watercress.

Slice veal across grain ¼ inch thick. Heat 1 tablespoon of the oil in a wide nonstick frying pan over high heat. Add about a fourth of the veal (do not crowd pan) and stir-fry until lightly browned (3 to 4 minutes). With a slotted spoon, remove veal from pan. Cook remaining veal, adding remaining 1 tablespoon oil as needed.

Prepare Mustard Sauce. Combine veal and sauce in a shallow 2- to 2½-quart casserole. Cover and bake in a 325° oven for 1 hour. Uncover and continue baking, stirring occasionally, until meat is tender when pierced (15 to 20 more minutes; sauce should be moist, but pan should contain little liquid). If made ahead, let cool, then cover and refrigerate until next day. Reheat, covered, in a 325° oven for about 40 minutes; if too dry, stir in 2 to 3 tablespoons water.

Just before serving, remove and discard tough watercress stems. Mea-

sure 4 cups sprigs, lightly packed. Seed and peel avocado and papaya; slice lengthwise into ¼-inch wedges. Coat avocado with lemon juice.

Alternate papaya and avocado wedges, dividing evenly, on 6 dinner plates. Arrange watercress alongside. Spoon veal onto watercress and garnish with lemon wedges. Makes 6 servings.

Mustard Sauce. In a medium-size bowl, combine 1 small **onion,** finely chopped; ⅓ cup **Dijon mustard;** 3 tablespoons **honey;** 2 tablespoons **soy sauce;** 1 tablespoon **raspberry or red wine vinegar;** 1 tablespoon chopped **fresh rosemary leaves** or 2 teaspoons dry rosemary; 1 tablespoon finely chopped **fresh ginger** or ½ teaspoon ground ginger; and ¾ teaspoon coarsely ground **black pepper.** Stir until blended.

Per serving: 32 grams protein, 20 grams carbohydrates, 27 grams total fat, 15 grams unsaturated fat, 107 milligrams cholesterol, 739 milligrams sodium.

POUNDED LAMB CHOPS WITH ROSEMARY

Preparation time: 10 minutes
Grilling time: About 4 minutes

Calories per serving: 451

4	**cloves garlic, minced or pressed**
2	**tablespoons minced fresh rosemary leaves or 1 tablespoon dry rosemary**
½	**cup minced parsley**
2	**tablespoons olive oil or salad oil**
4	**lamb rib or loin chops (¾ to 1 inch thick; about 1¼ lbs. *total*)**
	Vegetable oil cooking spray
	Fresh rosemary sprigs (optional)

To prepare these chops for speedy cooking on the grill, you first pound them until thin (the rib bone lies at one side, so you can leave it attached). A garlic-rosemary mixture rubbed into each chop produces a wonderful aroma during grilling.

In a small bowl, mix garlic, minced rosemary, parsley, and oil. Slash fat around each lamb chop at about 1-inch intervals. Rub about 1 tablespoon of the rosemary mixture on each side of each chop.

Place 1 or 2 chops between large pieces of plastic wrap. With a flat-

surfaced mallet, pound meat evenly and firmly until about ¼ inch thick. (At this point, you may cover and refrigerate for up to 8 hours.)

Spray a barbecue grill with cooking spray. Place chops on grill about 6 inches above a solid bed of hot coals. Grill, turning once, until done to your liking when slashed (about 4 minutes *total* for medium-rare). Garnish with rosemary sprigs, if desired. Makes 4 servings.

Per serving: 18 grams protein, 2 grams carbohydrates, 41 grams total fat, 19 grams unsaturated fat, 81 milligrams cholesterol, 64 milligrams sodium.

MONGOLIAN LAMB WITH SPRING ONIONS

Preparation time: About 15 minutes
Cooking time: 6 to 8 minutes

Calories per serving: 343

1	pound boneless leg of lamb
½	teaspoon Chinese five-spice
1	egg white
2	cloves garlic, slivered
4	thin slices fresh ginger or ⅛ teaspoon ground ginger
3	teaspoons cornstarch
5	teaspoons soy sauce
6	tablespoons dry sherry
2	tablespoons water
10	green onions (including tops)
2	tablespoons salad oil

This lightning-quick stir-fry gets its exotic flavor from a low-calorie combination of garlic, ginger, Chinese five-spice seasoning, and bright green onions. Serve it with steamed rice for an out-of-the-ordinary light meal.

Trim and discard any fat from lamb; slice into bite-size strips ⅛ inch thick. In a medium-size bowl, mix lamb, five-spice, egg white, garlic, ginger, 1 teaspoon of the cornstarch, and 1 teaspoon of the soy sauce. Let stand for 10 minutes.

Meanwhile, blend remaining 2 teaspoons cornstarch, remaining 4 teaspoons soy sauce, sherry, and water in a small bowl. Cut off white part of each onion, then cut in half; cut two 1½-inch-long sections from each green top, discarding remainder.

Heat oil in a wide nonstick frying pan over high heat. Add meat mixture and cook, stirring, until lightly browned (2 to 3 minutes). Return to bowl.

To pan add cornstarch mixture and white part of onions. Cook, stirring, until mixture thickens. Add meat mixture and onion tops and cook, stirring, just until heated through (1 to 2 minutes). Makes 4 servings.

Per serving: 22 grams protein, 6 grams carbohydrates, 25 grams total fat, 13 grams unsaturated fat, 81 milligrams cholesterol, 632 milligrams sodium.

LAMB PATTIES WITH MELON & MINT

(Pictured on page 99)

Preparation time: 20 minutes
Grilling time: 8 to 10 minutes

Calories per serving: 363

2	tablespoons slivered almonds
1	egg
¼	teaspoon salt
2	tablespoons fine dry bread crumbs
1	clove garlic, minced or pressed
1	large onion, finely chopped
⅓	cup minced fresh mint leaves
1	pound lean ground lamb
	Vegetable oil cooking spray
1	small cantaloupe, seeded, cut into 8 wedges, and peeled
	Orange wedges
	Fresh mint sprigs

Grill wedges of sweet cantaloupe alongside mint-seasoned ground lamb patties for a combination that's refreshingly different. A squeeze of juice from accompanying orange wedges adds a light lift.

Toast almonds in a small frying pan over medium-low heat, shaking pan often, until golden (about 7 minutes). Let cool.

In a large bowl, beat egg with salt. Add bread crumbs, garlic, onion, minced mint, almonds, and ground lamb, mixing lightly until well combined. Shape meat mixture into four ¾-inch-thick patties.

Spray a barbecue grill with cooking spray. Place melon wedges and meat patties on grill 4 to 6 inches above a solid bed of hot coals. Grill melon, turning often, just until hot (6 to 8 minutes *total*). Grill meat, turning once, until browned and done to your liking when slashed (about 8 minutes *total* for medium-rare).

Arrange lamb patties and orange wedges on a warm serving platter; garnish with mint sprigs. Offer melon wedges alongside. Makes 4 servings.

Per serving: 22 grams protein, 17 grams carbohydrates, 31 grams total fat, 13 grams unsaturated fat, 144 milligrams cholesterol, 253 milligrams sodium.

PORK CHOPS WITH ORANGE & MUSHROOM SAUCE

Preparation time: 10 minutes
Cooking time: About 45 minutes

Calories per serving: 429

1 pound boneless loin pork chops (about ¾ inch thick)

1 tablespoon butter or margarine

½ pound small mushrooms, halved

1 cup orange juice

1 tablespoon grated orange peel

¼ teaspoon salt

⅛ teaspoon white pepper

1½ teaspoons cornstarch

½ cup plain lowfat yogurt

Chopped parsley

Rich-tasting but not rich in calories, the sauce for this pork chop dish has a tangy yogurt base, enlivened by the fresh flavor of orange juice. For an easy meal, bake yams in their jackets to serve alongside.

Trim and discard fat from chops. In a wide nonstick frying pan, cook chops in their own drippings over medium-high heat, turning once, until browned (2 to 3 minutes *total*). Remove chops. Spoon off and discard any drippings.

Melt butter in pan. Add mushrooms and cook, stirring often, until mushrooms begin to brown (about 3 minutes). Stir in orange juice and orange peel. Return chops to pan and sprinkle with salt and pepper. Reduce heat, cover, and simmer until chops are tender when pierced (35 to 40 minutes).

With a slotted spoon, lift out chops and mushrooms, reserving liquid, and arrange on a warm serving platter; keep warm. Blend cornstarch and yogurt; add to liquid in pan. Cook over high heat, stirring, until sauce boils and thickens (about 5 minutes). Pour over chops and mushrooms; sprinkle with parsley. Makes 4 servings.

Per serving: 22 grams protein, 12 grams carbohydrates, 32 grams total fat, 16 grams unsaturated fat, 82 milligrams cholesterol, 260 milligrams sodium.

GRILLED GINGERED PORK CHOPS

Preparation time: 12 to 15 minutes
Marinating time: 4 hours or more
Grilling time: About 20 minutes

Calories per serving: 505

¼ cup minced fresh ginger or 1 tablespoon ground ginger

¾ cup dry sherry

2 cloves garlic, minced or pressed

3 tablespoons soy sauce

1 tablespoon *each* sugar and salad oil

4 loin pork chops (½ inch thick; about 1½ lbs. *total*)

1 head napa (Chinese) cabbage (about 2½ lbs.)

Vegetable oil cooking spray

A ginger-flavored sherry marinade adds interest to pork chops in this recipe. Wedges of napa cabbage, basted with the same marinade, grill alongside the chops on the barbecue.

In a large, shallow bowl, combine ginger, sherry, garlic, soy sauce, sugar, and oil; stir until sugar is dissolved.

Trim and discard fat from chops. Add to sherry mixture. Cover and refrigerate, turning chops occasionally, for at least 4 hours or until next day.

Cut cabbage lengthwise into quarters. Steam, covered, on a rack over boiling water just until barely wilted (about 5 minutes). If made ahead, let cool, then cover and refrigerate until next day.

Spray a barbecue grill with cooking spray. Lift out chops, reserving marinade, and place on grill 4 to 6 inches above a solid bed of medium coals. Brush with marinade and grill, turning once, until no longer pink when slashed (about 20 minutes *total*). Shortly after chops begin to brown, add cabbage quarters and grill, turning once and basting occasionally with any remaining marinade, until heated through (about 15 minutes *total*). Arrange chops and cabbage on a warm serving platter. Makes 4 servings.

Per serving: 27 grams protein, 17 grams carbohydrates, 37 grams total fat, 20 grams unsaturated fat, 83 milligrams cholesterol, 1137 milligrams sodium.

A fruitful idea for a light summertime meal
pairs minted, almond-studded ground lamb patties with sweet
cantaloupe slices on the grill. Juicy orange wedges and fresh mint leaves
garnish Lamb Patties with Melon & Mint (page 97).

L·I·G·H·T

Dessert! It's the part of the meal that everybody looks forward to—and devotees of light cuisine are no exception. Our dessert selection is proof positive that desserts don't have to be sinfully rich to be delightfully delicious. As you'll see, we've selected desserts that are not only a treat to eat but also are low in calories and, in many cases, full of essential nutrients.

From luscious hot or cold fruits to frosty sorbets to fluffy goodies from the oven, you'll find a range of dessert dishes to satisfy any taste.

Fabulous fresh fruits. The first place to look for sweet-tasting desserts that are naturally low in calories and high in vitamins is among the array of fresh fruits available now in every season. We offer you elegant ideas for serving such fruits as melon, berries, oranges, peaches, and pears.

Some, like Peach Brûlée (page 103) and Poached Pears in Ginger-Lemon Syrup (page 104), feature fruit that's lightly cooked. Others, such as Ginger-Nut Honeydew Wedges (facing page), are based on uncooked fruit.

Simple embellishments can enhance the natural good flavor of fresh fruit without adding lots of extra calories. For example, you can squeeze on lemon or lime juice to add sophisticated flavor at only 4 calories per tablespoon. Try drizzling on honey or dusting with brown sugar or powdered sugar, then serving the fruit at room temperature or broiling it briefly. Or how about sprinkling on some toasted sliced almonds, shredded coconut, or even a fruit-flavored liqueur?

Cool and frosty desserts. Instead of relying on rich, high-fat cream, our frozen desserts are based on lowfat milk or yogurt or, in the case of sorbets and ices, on a simple mixture of fruit juice or wine with sugar and water. The results are light and fresh-tasting.

One delicious example is tart-sweet Vanilla Frozen Yogurt (page 106). For something a little different, whip up smooth, rich-tasting Vanilla Tofulato (page 105), a unique and delightful tofu-based dessert with several flavor variations. Both recipes make use of an ice cream freezer (self-refrigerated, electric, or hand-cranked).

You can make other frozen desserts, such as Creamy Berry Sherbet (page 108) and golden Papaya Sorbet (page 109), in your freezer. For best results, it should be one that maintains a temperature of 0°F or colder.

Glorious desserts from the oven. Sometimes you just don't feel you've given dessert the attention it deserves unless you've baked something in the oven. For those occasions, we suggest billowy Salzburger Nockerln (page 110), a gorgeous soufflélike creation that's finished with a sprinkling of shaved chocolate. Or try Fluffy Lemon Cheesecake (page 109), a light and lemony version of a favorite indulgence.

Whether you choose a fresh-fruit, frozen, or baked delight, you'll find that a light dessert at the end of a meal can be a conclusion well worth waiting for.

Here's a selection of desserts that's all sweetness and light— from sugar-sparkled fresh melon and plump berries to sparkling frozen sorbets to fluffy, cloud-light creations from the oven. It's all here— except the calories.

D·E·S·S·E·R·T·S

GINGER-NUT HONEYDEW WEDGES

Preparation time: 12 to 15 minutes

Calories per serving: 141

¼ cup almonds

2 tablespoons *each* sugar and finely chopped candied ginger

1 honeydew melon (about 5 lbs.)

A sweet and crunchy sprinkling of toasted almonds, candied ginger, and just a little sugar enhances juicy melon wedges without adding many calories.

Spread almonds in a pie pan; toast in a 350° oven until golden under skin (7 to 8 minutes). Let cool slightly, then coarsely chop.

In a small bowl, combine toasted almonds, sugar, and ginger; mix until well blended. Cut melon into 6 equal-size wedges; remove and discard seeds. Arrange on dessert plates. Evenly sprinkle almond mixture over melon wedges. Makes 6 servings.

Per serving: 3 grams protein, 24 grams carbohydrates, 4 grams total fat, 3 grams unsaturated fat, 0 milligrams cholesterol, 30 milligrams sodium.

LIGHT TOUCHES: FRESH FRUIT FOR A LIGHT DESSERT

Simple fresh fruit provides an after-dinner nibble that's sweet and satisfying, as well as healthy. Here are the calorie counts for some favorites.

	Calories
Apple (2¾ inches in diameter)	80
Apricot (1¼ inches in diameter)	19
Banana (8¾ inches long)	101
Berries (½ cup blueberries, boysenberries, raspberries, or strawberries)	28–45
Cherries, sweet (½ cup)	41
Grapes, seedless (½ cup)	54
Melon (2-inch wedge of cantaloupe, casaba, or honeydew)	38–50
Orange (2½ inches in diameter)	64
Peach (2½ inches in diameter)	38
Pineapple (½ cup, diced)	41
Tangerine (2½ inches in diameter)	46

ITALIAN-STYLE MIXED BERRIES

Preparation time: 10 minutes

Calories per serving: 73

1 basket (about 3 cups) strawberries, hulled

1 basket (about 2 cups) raspberries

1 cup blueberries

Lemon wedges

Sugar (optional)

Fresh fruit is a classic Italian dessert. Here, it's a glorious mix of raspberries, blueberries, and strawberries, topped only with a squeeze of lemon. A sprinkle of sugar will add about 15 calories per teaspoon.

Rinse berries carefully and pat dry. Cut strawberries in half.

In a large glass bowl, lightly mix strawberries, raspberries, and blueberries. If made ahead, refrigerate for up to 4 hours. Serve berries with lemon wedges to squeeze over each serving; sprinkle with sugar, if desired. Makes 6 servings.

Per serving: 1 gram protein, 17 grams carbohydrates, .73 gram total fat, 0 grams unsaturated fat, 0 milligrams cholesterol, 2 milligrams sodium.

A heavenly cloud of meringue topped with
melting chocolate curls, Salzburger Nockerln (page 110)
is a sweet golden offering from Austria. You can indulge and still feel
angelic—one serving has just 134 calories.

PEACH BRÛLÉE

Preparation time: 20 to 25 minutes
Broiling time: 1½ to 2½ minutes

Calories per serving: 105

2 **tablespoons butter or margarine, melted**
2 **tablespoons lemon juice**
3 **large ripe peaches, halved, pitted, and peeled**
½ **cup blueberries**
Vegetable oil cooking spray
6 **tablespoons firmly packed brown sugar**
Fresh mint sprigs

Broiled with a caramelized crust of brown sugar, fresh peaches and blueberries make an irresistible light dessert.

In a shallow bowl, mix butter and lemon juice. Turn peach halves in butter mixture, then transfer, cut side up, to a large broiler pan. Fill each peach cavity with 1 tablespoon of the blueberries. Set aside.

Line a large baking sheet with foil and generously spray with cooking spray. Push 1 tablespoon of the brown sugar through a wire sieve onto foil to make an even layer about 3 inches square; repeat, making a total of 6 squares. Broil about 6 inches below heat until sugar is melted (1 to 2 minutes); watch carefully to avoid scorching. Let cool until set but still pliable (about 30 seconds).

With a wide spatula, set a sugar square on top of each peach half.

Broil about 6 inches below heat just until sugar crust drapes around peach (10 to 30 seconds). Transfer to small bowls. Garnish servings with mint and remaining berries. Serve immediately. Makes 6 servings.

Per serving: .6 gram protein, 18 grams carbohydrates, 4 grams total fat, 1 gram unsaturated fat, 12 milligrams cholesterol, 50 milligrams sodium.

ORANGES WITH CHAMPAGNE ZABAGLIONE

Preparation time: 15 minutes
Cooking time: About 5 minutes

Calories per serving: 175

2 **large oranges**
4 **egg yolks**
⅓ **cup sugar**
1 **cup champagne or other dry sparkling white wine**

Make this lighter-than-air Italian favorite even lighter by using champagne or other dry sparkling wine instead of the customary sweet marsala. Oranges add a fresh touch.

With a sharp knife, cut off peel and white membrane from oranges. Slice or section fruit. Place a fourth of the oranges in each of 4 stemmed dessert or wine glasses. Set aside. (At this point, you may let stand for up to 4 hours.)

In a round-bottomed zabaglione pan or in top of a double boiler, combine egg yolks, sugar, and ¾ cup of the champagne. Place zabaglione pan directly over medium-high heat (or set double boiler over boiling water). Cook, whipping constantly with a wire whisk or electric mixer,

until egg mixture is very foamy and thick enough to form a soft peak when beater is lifted (about 5 minutes). Remove from heat.

Immediately pour remaining ¼ cup champagne equally over oranges; pour zabaglione evenly over oranges. Makes 4 servings.

Per serving: 3 grams protein, 27 grams carbohydrates, 5 grams total fat, 3 grams unsaturated fat, 252 milligrams cholesterol, 13 milligrams sodium.

BROILED ORANGE HALVES

Preparation time: About 10 minutes
Broiling time: About 3 minutes

Calories per serving: 58

---

3 large oranges
1 tablespoon *each* firmly packed brown sugar and dry sherry
1 tablespoon butter or margarine, melted

Fresh oranges are warmed with a brown sugar topping for a quick and easy finale to almost any meal.

Cut oranges in half crosswise. With a grapefruit knife, cut around orange to separate fruit from peel and membrane, leaving fruit in shell. Arrange fruit, cut side up, in a 9-inch-square baking pan.

Sprinkle each orange half with ½ teaspoon *each* brown sugar, sherry, and butter. Broil 4 inches below heat until hot and bubbly (about 3 minutes). Serve warm to eat from shell with a spoon. Makes 6 servings.

Per serving: .67 gram protein, 10 grams carbohydrates, 2 grams total fat, .69 gram unsaturated fat, 6 milligrams cholesterol, 25 milligrams sodium.

LIGHT TOUCHES: SUGAR VS. SUGAR SUBSTITUTES

You'll notice that when we call for sweetener in our light dessert recipes, we've specified sugar (sucrose). One reason is that sugar substitutes vary in sweetness, making it difficult to specify an amount.

Another reason is that sugar often does more than simply sweeten a dessert. It helps to make baked products, such as cakes and cookies, tender. And because of surface caramelization, sugar aids in browning. Also, when you add sugar while beating egg whites to make a meringue or to leaven, the mixture becomes more stable.

POACHED PEARS IN GINGER-LEMON SYRUP

(Pictured on cover)

Preparation time: 15 minutes
Cooking time: 45 to 55 minutes
Chilling time: 1½ hours or more

Calories per serving: 144

---

1 lemon
1 tablespoon fresh ginger, cut into julienne strips
⅓ cup sugar
About 3 cups water
6 medium-size firm Bartlett or Anjou pears (2½ to 3 inches in diameter), peeled (leave stems attached)

Poach fresh whole pears in an infusion of ginger and lemon, then chill them to create an elegant dessert that's refreshingly light.

With a vegetable peeler, pare zest (colored outer layer of peel) from lemon. Cut peel into enough thin strips to make 1 tablespoon. Ream enough lemon to make 1 tablespoon juice.

In a 5- to 6-quart pan, combine lemon peel, lemon juice, ginger, sugar, and 3 cups of the water. Bring to a boil over high heat. Add pears and more water, if needed, to cover fruit. Reduce heat, cover, and simmer until pears are tender when pierced (20 to 30 minutes).

With a slotted spoon, transfer pears to 6 shallow rimmed dishes or bowls. Increase heat to high and boil syrup, uncovered, until reduced to 1 cup (about 25 minutes). Pour syrup over pears. Let cool; then cover and refrigerate until cold (about 1½ hours) or for up to 2 days. Makes 6 servings.

Per serving: 1 gram protein, 36 grams carbohydrates, .7 gram total fat, 0 grams unsaturated fat, 0 milligrams cholesterol, 4 milligrams sodium.

VANILLA TOFULATO

2 teaspoons unflavored gelatin (optional)

⅓ cup water (optional)

⅔ cup sugar

1 pound soft tofu (bean curd), drained

1½ cups buttermilk, plain yogurt, whole milk, or whipping cream

⅓ cup whipping cream

2 teaspoons vanilla

This happy meeting of Oriental tofu and Italian gelato results in a delicious, smooth-textured frozen dessert that's light and lean. Besides vanilla, we offer a wide range of flavors.

Our calorie count is for a half-cup serving of vanilla tofulato made with buttermilk (made with whole milk, a serving is about 165 calories). Tofulato melts quickly once it gets soft; adding gelatin helps stabilize it.

If using gelatin, combine gelatin and water in a small pan. Let stand until softened (about 5 minutes). Add sugar and place over medium heat, stirring until gelatin is completely dissolved. (If using a microwave oven, soften gelatin in water in a microwave-safe dish; microwave on **HIGH (100%)** for about 1 minute, stirring once.)

In a food processor or blender, whirl gelatin mixture (or just sugar if omitting gelatin) and tofu until smooth. Stir tofu mixture into buttermilk; add the ⅓ cup whipping cream and vanilla.

Pour into container of a 1-quart or larger self-refrigerated, electric, or hand-cranked ice cream maker. Process according to manufacturer's directions. Serve when just frozen, or firm for 1 to 2 more hours in a freezer. For best flavor, keep for no more than 3 weeks.

If solidly frozen, let tofulato stand at room temperature for about 30 minutes before serving. Makes 8 servings (about 1 quart).

Per serving: 7 grams protein, 19 grams carbohydrates, 6 grams total fat, 1 gram unsaturated fat, 14 milligrams cholesterol, 144 milligrams sodium.

Banana Tofulato

Prepare Vanilla Tofulato, using buttermilk or yogurt and the ⅓ cup whipping cream. With whipping cream and vanilla, add ⅓ cup mashed ripe **banana.** Makes 8 servings (160 calories per serving).

Ginger or Ginger-Banana Tofulato

Prepare Vanilla Tofulato, using buttermilk or yogurt and the ⅓ cup whipping cream. With whipping cream and vanilla, add ⅓ cup finely chopped **candied ginger** and, if desired, ⅓ cup mashed ripe **banana.** (Mashed ripe, peeled peach or pear can be substituted for banana.) Makes 8 servings (165 calories per serving).

Fresh Berry Tofulato

Purée 1½ cups **berries** (strawberries, raspberries, olallieberries, boysenberries, or blueberries) with 3 tablespoons **sugar.** If desired, rub purée through a wire strainer to remove any seeds.

In a 2- to 3-quart pan, bring purée to a boil over medium-high heat. Reduce heat to maintain a gentle boil and cook, uncovered, stirring often, until fruit is reduced to ½ cup (about 20 minutes). Stir in 2 teaspoons **lemon juice.**

Prepare Vanilla Tofulato, using buttermilk or yogurt and the ⅓ cup whipping cream. With whipping cream and vanilla, add berry purée. Makes 8 servings (180 calories per serving).

Tofulato Black & White

Prepare Vanilla Tofulato. For each serving, pour steaming-hot **espresso** or other full-flavored black coffee into a large mug. Add a scoop of tofulato. Serve to eat with a spoon or to drink. Makes 12 servings (101 calories per serving).

VANILLA FROZEN YOGURT

1 envelope unflavored gelatin

½ cup whole milk

2 eggs, separated, or 2 egg whites

3 cups plain lowfat yogurt

¾ cup sugar; or ⅓ cup honey and ¼ cup sugar

2 tablespoons vanilla

Frozen yogurt, a deservedly popular summer dessert, is as luscious as it is light and cool. To make it lighter still, prepare it with egg whites instead of whole eggs.

In a small pan, combine gelatin and milk; let stand until softened (about 5 minutes). Place over medium heat, stirring until gelatin is completely dissolved. (If using a microwave oven, soften gelatin in milk in a microwave-safe dish; microwave on **HIGH (100%)** for about 1 minute, stirring once.) Let cool for about 5 minutes.

If using whole eggs, beat yolks lightly with a wire whisk in a large bowl. Beat in yogurt and ½ cup of the sugar (or the ⅓ cup honey) until smoothly blended. Beat in gelatin mixture and vanilla.

In a medium-size bowl, beat egg whites until soft peaks form; gradually add remaining ¼ cup sugar, beating until stiff and glossy. Fold into yogurt mixture.

Pour into container of a 2-quart or larger self-refrigerated, electric, or hand-cranked ice cream maker. Process according to manufacturer's directions. Serve when just frozen or cover and store in your freezer.

If solidly frozen, let frozen yogurt stand at room temperature for about 30 minutes before serving. Makes 10 servings (about 1¼ quarts).

Per serving: 5 grams protein, 19 grams carbohydrates, 3 grams total fat, 1 gram unsaturated fat, 58 milligrams cholesterol, 54 milligrams sodium.

Fresh Berry Frozen Yogurt

Rinse about 1 pint **strawberries,** raspberries, or olallieberries. Mash well or whirl in a blender or food processor until coarsely crushed; you should have 1½ cups. Add ½ cup **sugar;** let stand until juices form. Spoon off and reserve ½ cup of the juice.

Follow directions for Vanilla Frozen Yogurt, substituting the ½ cup berry juice for milk to dissolve gelatin. Omit ½ cup of the sugar and vanilla; add 2 tablespoons **lemon juice,** sweetened berries, and any remaining juices to yogurt mixture. Makes 16 servings (76 calories per serving).

Fresh Peach, Nectarine, or Apricot Frozen Yogurt

Remove and discard pits from peeled ripe **peaches** or unpeeled nectarines or apricots. In a blender or food processor, whirl fruit until coarsely crushed; you should have 1½ cups. Add ½ cup **sugar** and 2 tablespoons **lemon juice;** let stand until juices form. Spoon off and reserve ½ cup of the juice.

Follow directions for Vanilla Frozen Yogurt, substituting the ½ cup fruit juice for milk to dissolve gelatin and preparing yogurt mixture without sugar. Add sweetened fruit to yogurt mixture; taste, then add up to ¼ cup more **sugar** if necessary. Omit vanilla, substituting ⅛ to ¼ teaspoon **almond extract.** Makes 16 servings (76 calories per serving).

Banana-Lime Frozen Yogurt

Follow directions for Vanilla Frozen Yogurt, substituting 1 can (6 oz.) **frozen limeade or lemonade concentrate** (thawed) for milk to dissolve gelatin. Omit vanilla and add 1 cup (about 2 large) mashed ripe **bananas** and, if desired, ⅓ cup **dark rum** to yogurt mixture. After mixture is frozen, stir in about ½ cup **sweetened flaked or shredded coconut.** Makes 16 servings (126 calories per serving).

CABERNET SAUVIGNON ICE

Preparation time: 15 to 20 minutes
Chilling time: 1 hour or more
Freezing time: 7 hours or more

Calories per serving: 156

| ¾ cup sugar |
| 1 cup water |
| 1½ cups *each* cabernet sauvignon and white grape juice |
| ¾ cup lemon juice |

Cabernet sauvignon gives this frosty-cool ice a refreshing sweet-tart flavor. If you wish, garnish with mint sprigs.

In a 1- to 1½-quart pan, combine sugar, water, and wine. Bring to a boil over high heat, then reduce heat and simmer gently, uncovered, for 5 minutes. Remove from heat and let stand for 10 minutes. Add grape juice and lemon juice; cover and refrigerate until cold (about 1 hour).

Pour mixture into 2 or 3 divided ice cube trays or a shallow 9-inch-square metal pan. Freeze until solid (about 4 hours). If frozen in pan, let stand at room temperature until you can break ice into chunks with a spoon.

Place ice, a third to half at a time, in a food processor; whirl, using short on-off pulses at first to break up cubes, then process continuously until mixture becomes a velvety slush (or beat all the ice with an electric mixer, starting slowly, then gradually increasing speed to high). Spoon ice into a container. Cover and freeze until solid (3 to 4 hours) or for up to a month. Makes 6 servings (about 5 cups).

Per serving: .28 gram protein, 40 grams carbohydrates, .06 gram total fat, 0 grams unsaturated fat, 0 milligrams cholesterol, 5 milligrams sodium.

CHAMPAGNE-CINNAMON SNOWBALL SHERBET

Preparation time: 15 minutes
Cooking time: About 10 minutes
Chilling time: 1½ to 2 hours
Freezing time: 14 hours or more

Calories per serving: 136

| ½ cup sugar |
| 1 cup water |
| 2 cinnamon sticks (*each* 3 inches long) |
| 2 cups champagne or other dry to sweet sparkling white wine |
| 2 tablespoons lemon juice |
| **Italian Meringue** (recipe follows) |
| 6 additional 3-inch cinnamon sticks, broken in half (optional) |

This sherbet gets its pale coolness from a champagne syrup blended and frozen with an airy meringue.

In a 1- to 2-quart pan, combine sugar, water, and the 2 cinnamon sticks. Boil, stirring, over high heat until syrup reaches 210°F on a thermometer (about 5 minutes). Remove from heat; stir in champagne and lemon juice. Refrigerate for 1½ to 2 hours. Meanwhile, prepare Italian Meringue; refrigerate.

Pour champagne syrup through a wire strainer into a 9-inch-square metal pan. Discard cinnamon sticks. Cover and freeze until softly but evenly frozen (at least 8 hours).

With a heavy spoon, break up frozen mixture and stir until slushy. Fold into cold meringue mixture until well combined. Cover tightly and freeze for 2 to 3 hours, folding occasionally to keep mixture evenly blended.

Freeze until firm (at least 4 hours) or for up to 3 months.

With an ice cream scoop, shape sherbet into ⅓-cup balls. Serve 2 scoops in each of 12 stemmed glasses or bowls; garnish with additional cinnamon sticks, if desired. Makes 12 servings (about 2 quarts).

Italian Meringue. In a 1- to 2-quart pan, mix 1 cup **sugar** and ½ cup **water**. Boil, uncovered, over medium-high heat until syrup reaches 228°F on a thermometer (about 5 minutes).

Meanwhile, in large bowl of an electric mixer, beat **4 egg whites** until soft peaks form. Beating constantly, slowly pour hot syrup in a thin, steady stream into egg whites (avoid hitting beaters) until stiff and glossy. Cover and refrigerate for at least 1 hour or for up to a day.

Per serving: 1 gram protein, 27 grams carbohydrates, 0 grams total fat, 0 grams unsaturated fat, 0 milligrams cholesterol, 18 milligrams sodium.

TROPICAL FRUIT GELATO

Preparation time: 20 minutes
Cooking time: About 20 minutes
Chilling time: 1½ to 2 hours
Freezing time: Depends on ice cream maker

Calories per serving: 172

3	cups lowfat milk
¾	cup sugar
6	egg yolks
1	teaspoon vanilla
2	cups fresh pineapple chunks
2	small ripe bananas (½ lb. *total*), cut into chunks
1	teaspoon grated orange peel
3	tablespoons orange juice

Pineapple, banana, and orange lend a taste of the tropics to this custardy homemade ice cream.

In a 3- to 4-quart pan, combine milk and sugar. Place over medium heat, stirring just until sugar is dissolved. With a wire whisk, gradually beat 1 cup of the warm milk mixture into egg yolks in a medium-size bowl, then beat egg mixture into remaining milk mixture.

Cook, stirring constantly, over medium-low heat until liquid coats back of a spoon (10 to 15 minutes). Remove from heat, stir in vanilla, and let cool slightly. Refrigerate until thoroughly chilled (1½ to 2 hours).

In a blender or food processor, combine pineapple, bananas, orange peel, and orange juice; whirl until puréed. Stir into chilled egg mixture.

Pour into container of a self-refrigerated, electric, or hand-cranked ice cream maker. Process according to manufacturer's directions. Serve when just frozen or store in your freezer for up to a month.

If solidly frozen, let gelato stand at room temperature for about 30 minutes before serving. Makes 10 servings (about 2 quarts).

Per serving: 5 grams protein, 28 grams carbohydrates, 5 grams total fat, 2 grams unsaturated fat, 158 milligrams cholesterol, 51 milligrams sodium.

CREAMY BERRY SHERBET

Preparation time: About 20 minutes
Freezing time: 2 to 3 hours

Calories per serving: 112

1	cup milk
1	cup raspberries, blackberries, olallieberries, or boysenberries
¼	cup sugar

With a tray of frozen milk cubes on hand in your freezer, you can whip up this refreshing fruit ice in minutes. Just blend the milk with berries and a little sugar in your food processor—and dessert's ready!

Pour milk into a divided ice cube tray; freeze solidly (2 to 3 hours). Refrigerate berries until thoroughly chilled; or freeze berries.

Shortly before serving, remove frozen milk and berries (if frozen) from freezer. Let stand at room temperature for 5 minutes. Remove milk cubes from tray (cut cubes into small chunks if large). Place cubes, about a third at a time, in a food processor; whirl, using short on-off pulses at first to break up cubes, then process continuously until velvety. Add berries, about a third at a time, and sugar; process until smooth.

To prepare without a food processor, place milk cubes, all at once, in large bowl of an electric mixer; break up with a wooden spoon. Beat, starting slowly, then gradually increasing speed to high. Purée berries with sugar in a blender (use 2 to 4 tablespoons of the milk slush to add more liquid, if necessary). Beat berry purée into milk slush.

Serve immediately; or spoon into a container and freeze until sherbet reaches desired firmness. If leftover sherbet is frozen, let stand at room temperature for 15 to 30 minutes before serving. Makes 4 servings (about 3 cups).

Per serving: 3 grams protein, 21 grams carbohydrates, 3 grams total fat, .77 gram unsaturated fat, 9 milligrams cholesterol, 31 milligrams sodium.

PAPAYA SORBET

Preparation time: About 20 minutes
Freezing time: 3½ hours or more

Calories per serving: 150

½ cup *each* sugar and water

1 cup peeled, seeded, and cubed papaya

2½ tablespoons lime juice

This exotic golden fruit ice is surprisingly simple to make. Fresh papaya, lime juice, and a little sugar are all it takes.

In a 1- to 2-quart pan, combine sugar and water. Bring to a boil over high heat; boil, uncovered, until reduced to ½ cup (about 5 minutes). Remove from heat and let cool.

In a blender or food processor, combine papaya and lime juice. Whirl until smoothly puréed. Mix in cooled syrup. If desired, pour fruit mixture through a fine wire strainer to remove any fibers. Pour into a 9-inch-square metal pan.

Cover and freeze just until almost firm (1½ to 2 hours). Break mixture into small pieces and transfer to large bowl of an electric mixer. Beat until slushy. Spoon sorbet into a container. Cover and freeze until firm (about 2 hours) or for up to a month.

Let stand at room temperature for 10 to 15 minutes before serving. Makes 3 servings (about 1½ cups).

Per serving: .27 gram protein, 39 grams carbohydrates, .03 gram total fat, 0 grams unsaturated fat, 0 milligrams cholesterol, 2 milligrams sodium.

FLUFFY LEMON CHEESECAKE

Preparation time: 30 minutes
Baking/standing time: 2 hours
Chilling time: 2 to 3 hours

Calories per serving: 167

Zwieback Crumb Crust (recipe follows)

Vegetable oil cooking spray

2 cups lowfat cottage cheese

¼ cup mild honey

4 eggs, separated

1 teaspoon grated lemon peel

2 tablespoons lemon juice

1 teaspoon vanilla

1 cup plain lowfat yogurt

½ cup sugar

Sliced strawberries or paper-thin lemon slices

Good news! There *is* a light cheesecake, and it's easy to make. Lowfat cottage cheese and yogurt, along with billowy beaten egg whites, make the lemony filling extra light.

Prepare Zwieback Crumb Crust. Spray a 9-inch spring-form pan with cooking spray. Pat crumb mixture evenly and firmly over bottom of pan. Bake in a 350° oven until lightly browned (8 to 10 minutes). Let cool on a wire rack. Reduce oven temperature to 300°.

In a blender or food processor, combine cottage cheese, honey, egg yolks, lemon peel, lemon juice, vanilla, and yogurt. Whirl until smooth. In a large bowl, beat egg whites until soft peaks form; gradually add sugar, beating until stiff and glossy. Fold in cheese mixture until blended. Spread lightly over crust.

Bake for 1 hour. Turn heat off, leaving cheesecake in oven for 1 more hour. Let cool, then refrigerate until thoroughly chilled (2 to 3 hours). Garnish with berries. Makes 12 servings.

Zwieback Crumb Crust. Crush 2 ounces **zwieback** (⅓ of a 6-oz. pkg.); you should have about ½ cup fine crumbs. In a medium-size bowl, combine crumbs, 2 tablespoons firmly packed **brown sugar,** and 2 tablespoons **butter** or margarine, melted. Mix until well combined.

Per serving: 9 grams protein, 22 grams carbohydrates, 5 grams total fat, 2 grams unsaturated fat, 95 milligrams cholesterol, 219 milligrams sodium.

SALZBURGER NOCKERLN

(Pictured on page 102)

1	ounce semisweet chocolate
4	eggs, separated
¼	cup sugar
4	teaspoons flour
1	tablespoon butter or margarine

Preparation time: 15 to 20 minutes
Baking time: 10 to 12 minutes

Calories per serving: 134

This ethereal dessert creation is a favorite in Austria and Bavaria. At home, your guests will applaud when you present it warm and golden from the oven.

Using a vegetable peeler, shave chocolate or make chocolate curls; set aside.

In large bowl of an electric mixer, beat egg whites until soft peaks form. Gradually add sugar, beating until very stiff. Set aside.

With same beater, beat egg yolks at high speed in a small bowl until very light in color and slightly thickened. Gradually add flour, beating until mixture is thick and well blended. Fold yolks into whites, blending lightly but thoroughly.

Quickly melt butter in a shallow oval or rectangular pan about 7 by 11 inches over direct medium heat. Making 6 equal mounds, heap egg mixture into warm pan. Bake in a 350° oven until top is pale brown (10 to 12 minutes). Sprinkle with chocolate and serve immediately. Makes 6 servings.

Per serving: 5 grams protein, 11 grams carbohydrates, 8 grams total fat, 4 grams unsaturated fat, 175 milligrams cholesterol, 64 milligrams sodium.

CUSTARD WITH CRISP SUGAR & BERRIES

3	cups lowfat milk
4	eggs
⅔	cup sugar
1	teaspoon vanilla
	Vegetable oil cooking spray
2	cups sliced strawberries

Preparation time: About 30 minutes
Baking time: 25 to 35 minutes

Calories per serving: 239

Dress up this homemade vanilla custard with a drizzle of golden caramel and a bright garnish of fresh strawberries.

In a 1- to 2-quart pan, warm milk over medium heat until steaming. In a large bowl, beat eggs, ⅓ cup of the sugar, and vanilla. Gradually stir in hot milk.

Spray six 1- to 1½-cup ramekins or custard cups with cooking spray. Place ramekins in a wide, deep baking pan. Pour custard mixture evenly into ramekins, then pour enough simmering water into baking pan so water is at same level as custard.

Bake, uncovered, in a 350° oven until custard jiggles only slightly in center when dish is gently shaken (25 to 35 minutes). Immediately remove custard from hot water and let cool for about 15 minutes. (At this point, you may cool completely, cover, and refrigerate until next day; use a paper towel to gently blot any moisture from top of custards.)

In a medium-size frying pan, melt remaining ⅓ cup sugar over medium heat, shaking pan often, until sugar is liquefied and amber in color (3 to 5 minutes).

Drizzle caramelized sugar equally over each custard. Garnish each with a few strawberry slices and serve immediately. Pass remaining berries to spoon over individual servings. Makes 6 servings.

Per serving: 10 grams protein, 36 grams carbohydrates, 7 grams total fat, 3 grams unsaturated fat, 180 milligrams cholesterol, 117 milligrams sodium.

I·N·D·E·X

A

Almond flatbread, 17
Anchovy dressing, 28
Apple Dutch baby, cinnamon-, 41
Apple yogurt salad, 26
Apricot, fresh, frozen yogurt, 106
Artichoke-olive soufflé, 46
Asian-style pasta primavera, 38
Asparagus, marinated, with sesame, 33
Asparagus & egg ramekins, 45
Asparagus & shrimp dijonnaise, 29
Asparagus chicken stir-fry, 70
Avocado-stuffed tomato salad, 23

B

Baked broccoli frittata, 46
Baked spinach crêpes, 38
Banana-lime frozen yogurt, 106
Banana tofulato, 105
Banana tofulato, ginger-, 105
Bandiera Italiana, 60
Barbecue-roasted chicken, 80
Barbecued chicken, herbed, 68
Barbecued turkey, 80
Barbecued turkey breast steaks, 82
Barley soup, chicken, 16
Basil, chicken, lemon, 73
Basil dressing, steeped chicken with, 76
Basil omelet, cheese &, 43
Bay leaves, grilled chicken with, 77
Beef
    burgers, oven-barbecued, 89
    burgundy, 88
    chiles rellenos meatballs, 90
    fajitas, 87
    flank steak, sweet-sour, 85
    hot, & watercress salad, 87
    lettuce tacos, 89
    patties, ground, with lemon sauce, 88
    pizza, ground, 90
    salad, tostada, 33
Beef & vegetable sauté, 85
Berries, custard with crisp sugar &, 110
Berries, mixed, Italian-style, 101
Berry, fresh, frozen yogurt, 106
Berry, fresh, tofulato, 105
Berry sherbet, creamy, 108
Biarritz sandwiches, 34
Breads
    almond flatbread, 17
    Moroccan sesame rusks, 17
Broccoli frittata, baked, 46
Broiled baby salmon with sherry-soy butter, 49
Broiled chicken with peaches, 68
Broiled orange halves, 104
Broth, fresh pea & pasta, 10
Bulgur stir-fry, vegetable &, 37
Burgers, oven-barbecued beef, 89
Burgers, vegetable, with peanut sauce, 39
Burgundy beef, 88
Butterflied trout with orange, 52

C

Cabernet sauvignon ice, 107
Cacciatore presto, chicken, 67
Calico stuffed trout, 52
Caper sauce, sautéed monkfish with, 51
Caper sauce, tangy, chicken with, 69
Carbohydrates, 5
Carrot & sweet pepper salsa, 92
Carrots & wild rice, herbed, 35
Champagne-cinnamon snowball sherbet, 107

Champagne zabaglione, oranges with, 103
Cheese & basil omelet, 43
Cheesecake, fluffy lemon, 109
Cheeses, choosing, 44
Chicken
    barbecue-roasted, 80
    barbecued, herbed, 68
    broiled, Oriental, 74
    broiled, with peaches, 68
    & grapes, garlic, 77
    grilled, with bay leaves, 77
    grilled Asian, 72
    grilled garlic-orange, 67
    lemon basil, 73
    Mexican soup with condiments, 15
    minted, & pineapple salad, 32
    & pasta, Mediterranean, 79
    roast, cilantro & sake, 65
    roast, poppy seed, 65
    salad, two-grape, 31
    salad sandwiches, crunchy, 34
    sesame, 72
    steeped, with basil dressing, 76
    stir-fry, asparagus, 70
    thighs, chutney-glazed, 79
    when to skin, 72
Chicken & garlic stir-fry, 74
Chicken barley soup, 16
Chicken cacciatore presto, 67
Chicken-noodle yogurt soup, 16
Chicken salad with spiced sesame sauce, 31
Chicken with a pocketful of mushrooms, 73
Chicken with happy spices, 69
Chicken with spinach & tomatoes, 70
Chicken with tangy caper sauce, 69
Chile vinegar, shrimp & jicama with, 29
Chiles rellenos meatballs, 90
Chive dressing, 23
Chutney, fresh parsley, 25
Chutney-glazed chicken thighs, 79
Cilantro & sake roast chicken, 65
Cilantro slaw, 21
Cilantro vinaigrette, 33
Cinnamon-apple Dutch baby, 41
Cinnamon snowball sherbet, champagne-, 107
Cool curry turkey salad, 32
Cranberry vinaigrette dressing, 25
Cream sauce, lemon-garlic, 93
Creamy berry sherbet, 108
Crêpes, spinach, baked, 38
Crunchy chicken salad sandwiches, 34
Crusty fish with yogurt-dill sauce, 59
Cucumber & mixed herb salsa, 93
Cucumber plate, salmon &, 56
Cucumber salad, tomato &, 23
Curry mayonnaise, steeped turkey with, 76
Curry turkey salad, cool, 32
Custard with crisp sugar & berries, 110

D

Deviled tofu salad sandwiches, 34
Dijon dressing, 28
Dill dressing, lemon-, vegetables with, 36
Dill sauce, yogurt-, crusty fish with, 59
Dressings, salad, 25, 26
Dutch baby, cinnamon-apple, 41

E

Eating light when dining out, 60
Egg ramekins, asparagus &, 45
Eggs, scrambled, Greek, 44

F

Fajitas, 87
Fats, 5
Fish
    bandiera Italian, 60
    crusty, with yogurt-dill sauce, 59
    fillets, parchment-baked, 53
    fillets or steaks, steam-poached, 61
    halibut, grilled, soy-lemon, 59
    layered Niçoise salad, 28

Fish (cont'd.)
    lean & fat, 53
    monkfish, sautéed, with caper sauce, 51
    salmon, broiled baby, with sherry-soy butter; 49
    salmon & cucumber plate, 56
    salmon with vegetable crest, 49
    seviche salad, 28
    skewers, Yugoslavian, 54
    sole, marinated, with vegetables, 57
    stew, tomatillo, 13
    trout, butterflied, with orange, 52
    trout, stuffed, calico, 52
    tuna, grilled, with teriyaki fruit sauce, 51
    tuna pie with spinach-rice crust, 57
    whole, steam-poached, 61
    See also Shellfish
Fish & vegetable skewers, 54
Flank steak, sweet-sour, 85
Flatbread, almond, 17
Fluffy lemon cheesecake, 109
Fresh berry frozen yogurt, 106
Fresh berry tofulato, 105
Fresh parsley chutney, 25
Fresh pea & pasta broth, 10
Fresh peach, nectarine, or apricot frozen yogurt, 106
Fresh tomato salsa, 92
Frittata, broccoli, baked, 46
Frozen yogurt
    banana-lime, 106
    fresh berry, 106
    fresh peach, nectarine, or apricot, 106
    vanilla, 106
Fruit, fresh, calories in, 101
Fruit, tropical, salsa, 93
Fruit sauce, teriyaki, grilled tuna with 51
Frying-pan scallops, 60

G

Game hens, grilled, with jalapeño jelly glaze, 81
Garden gazpacho, 9
Garlic chicken & grapes, 77
Garlic cream sauce, lemon-, 93
Garlic-orange chicken, grilled, 67
Garlic stir-fry, chicken &, 74
Gazpacho, garden, 9
Gelato, tropical fruit, 108
Ginger-banana tofulato, 105
Ginger-lemon syrup, poached pears in, 104
Ginger-nut honeydew wedges, 101
Ginger or ginger-banana tofulato, 105
Ginger steamed mussels, sesame-, 12
Gingered pork chops, grilled, 98
Grapes, garlic chicken &, 77
Greek peasant salad, 24
Greek scrambled eggs, 44
Green or gold pepper dressing, 25
Green pea salad, 26
Greens with oranges, 21
Grilled Asian chicken, 72
Grilled chicken with bay leaves, 77
Grilled game hens with jalapeño jelly glaze, 81
Grilled garlic-orange chicken, 67
Grilled gingered pork chops, 98
Grilled soy-lemon halibut, 59
Grilled tuna with teriyaki fruit sauce, 51
Grilled veal chops with lemon & thyme, 95
Ground beef patties with lemon sauce, 88
Ground beef pizza, 90
Ground turkey sauce with spaghetti squash, 81

H

Halibut, grilled soy-lemon, 59
Herb salsa, mixed, cucumber &, 93
Herbed barbecued chicken, 68
Herbed carrots & wild rice, 35

Herbed tomato sauce, 39
Honey-poppy seed dressing, 25
Honeydew wedges, ginger-nut, 101
Hot beef & watercress salad, 87

I

Ice, cabernet sauvignon, 107
Italian-style mixed berries, 101

J

Jalapeño jelly glaze, grilled game hens with, 81
Jicama, shrimp &, with chile vinegar, 29

L

Lamb
    chops, pounded, with rosemary, 96
    Mongolian, with spring onions, 97
Lamb patties with melon & mint, 97
Lamb-stuffed meatball soup, 18
Layered Niçoise salad, 28
Lemon & thyme, grilled veal chops with, 95
Lemon basil chicken, 73
Lemon cheesecake, fluffy, 109
Lemon-dill dressing, vegetables with, 36
Lemon dressing, 24
Lemon-garlic cream sauce, 93
Lemon halibut, grilled soy-, 59
Lemon sauce, ground beef patties with, 88
Lemon syrup, ginger-, poached pears in, 104
Lettuce tacos, 89
Lime frozen yogurt, banana-, 106
Lime-garlic dressing, 21

M

Marinated asparagus with sesame, 33
Marinated sole with vegetables, 57
Matchstick zucchini, 36
Mayonnaise, curry, steeped turkey with, 76
Meatball soup, lamb-stuffed, 18
Meatballs, chiles rellenos, 90
Mediterranean chicken & pasta, 79
Melon & mint, lamb patties with, 97
Menus, 7
Meringue, Italian, 107
Mexican soup with condiments, 15
Milk products, 13
Mint, melon &, lamb patties with, 97
Minted chicken & pineapple salad, 32
Mongolian lamb with spring onions, 97
Monkfish, sautéed, with caper sauce, 51
Moroccan sesame rusks, 17
Mushroom & vegetable soup, 10
Mushroom-crust quiche, 45
Mushroom sauce, orange & pork chops with, 98
Mushrooms, chicken with a pocketful of, 73
Mushrooms, turkey scaloppine with, 82
Mussels, sesame-ginger steamed, 12
Mustard-glazed veal strips, 96
Mustard sauce, 96

N

Nectarine, fresh, frozen yogurt, 106
Niçoise salad, layered, 28
Noodle yogurt soup, chicken-, 16
Nut honeydew wedges, ginger-, 101

O

Olive soufflé, artichoke-, 46
Omelet(s)
    cheese & basil, 43
    zucchini, 44
Omelet with julienne vegetables, 43

Onions, spring, Mongolian lamb with, 97
Orange, butterflied trout with, 52
Orange & mushroom sauce, pork chops with, 98
Orange chicken, grilled garlic-, 67
Orange halves, broiled, 104
Oranges, greens with, 21
Oranges with champagne zabaglione, 103
Oriental broiled chicken, 74
Oven-barbecued beef burgers, 89

P

Pancakes, ricotta, 41
Papaya sorbet, 109
Parchment-baked fish fillets, 53
Parchment-baked shrimp & pesto, 62
Parsley chutney, fresh, 25
Pasta
    bandiera Italiana, 60
    broth, fresh pea &, 10
    Mediterranean chicken &, 79
    primavera, Asian-style, 38
    salad, spring harvest, 24
Pea, fresh, & pasta broth, 10
Pea, green, salad, 26
Pea pods, scallops with, 56
Peach, fresh, frozen yogurt, 106
Peach brûlée, 103
Peaches, broiled chicken with, 68
Peanut sauce, vegetable burgers with, 39
Pears, poached, in ginger-lemon syrup, 104
Peas, veal sauté with, 95
Peking sauce, stir-fried shrimp with, 62
Pepper dressing, green or gold, 25
Peppers, turkey scaloppine with, 82
Pesto, shrimp &, parchment-baked, 62
Pineapple salad, minted chicken &, 32
Pizza, ground beef, 90
Poached pears in ginger-lemon syrup, 104
Poppy seed dressing, honey-, 25
Poppy seed roast chicken, 65
Pork chops, gingered, grilled, 98
Pork chops with orange & mushroom sauce, 98
Potatoes, new, roasted, 37
Pounded lamb chops with rosemary, 96
Protein, 5

Q

Quiche, mushroom-crust, 45

R

Rice, wild, herbed carrots &, 35
Rice crust, spinach-, tuna pie with, 57
Ricotta pancakes, 41
Roast chicken, cilantro & sake, 65
Roast chicken, poppy seed, 65
Roasted new potatoes, 37
Roasted salsa, 92
Rosemary, pounded lamb chops with, 96
Rusks, Moroccan sesame, 17

S

Sake roast chicken, cilantro &, 65
Salad(s)
    apple yogurt, 26
    asparagus, marinated, with sesame, 33
    asparagus & shrimp dijonnaise, 29
    avocado-stuffed tomato, 23
    beef, hot, & watercress, 87
    chicken, crunchy, sandwiches, 34
    chicken, minted, & pineapple, 32
    chicken, with spiced sesame sauce, 31
    chicken, steeped, with basil dressing, 76

Salad(s) (cont'd.)
    chicken, two-grape, 31
    cilantro slaw, 21
    Greek peasant, 24
    green pea, 26
    greens with oranges, 21
    layered Niçoise, 28
    pasta, spring harvest, 24
    seviche, 28
    shrimp & jicama with chile vinegar, 29
    sole, marinated, with vegetables, 57
    tofu, deviled, sandwiches, 34
    tomato & cucumber, 23
    tostada beef, 33
    turkey, cool curry, 32
    turkey, steeped, with curry mayonnaise, 76
Salmon, broiled baby, with sherry-soy butter, 49
Salmon & cucumber plate, 56
Salmon with vegetable crest, 49
Salsa
    carrot & sweet pepper, 92
    cucumber & mixed herb, 93
    fresca, 87
    fresh tomato, 92
    roasted, 92
    tropical fruit, 93
Salzburger nockerln, 110
Sandwiches
    Biarritz, 34
    crunchy chicken salad, 34
    deviled tofu salad, 34
Sauces, slimming, 92–93
Sautéed monkfish with caper sauce, 51
Scallops
    bandiera Italiana, 60
    frying-pan, 60
Scallops with pea pods, 56
Sesame, marinated asparagus with, 33
Sesame chicken, 72
Sesame-ginger steamed mussels, 12
Sesame rusks, Moroccan, 17
Sesame sauce, spiced, chicken salad with, 31
Seviche salad, 28
Shellfish
    asparagus & shrimp dijonnaise, 29
    bandiera Italiana, 60
    mussels, steamed, sesame-ginger, 12
    scallops, frying-pan, 60
    scallops with pea pods, 56
    shrimp, stir-fried, with Peking sauce, 62
    shrimp drop soup, 15
    shrimp & jicama with chile vinegar, 29
    shrimp & pesto, parchment-baked, 62
Sherbet, champagne-cinnamon snowball, 107
Sherbet, creamy berry, 108
Sherry-soy butter, broiled baby salmon with, 49
Sherry-soy sauce, 43
Shrimp
    dijonnaise, asparagus &, 29
    & pesto, parchment-baked, 62
    stir-fried, with Peking sauce, 62
Shrimp & jicama with chile vinegar, 29
Shrimp drop soup, 15
Slaw, cilantro, 21
Sodium, 5, 21
Sole, marinated, with vegetables, 57
Sorbet, papaya, 109
Soufflé, artichoke-olive, 46
Soups
    chicken barley, 16
    chicken-noodle yogurt, 16
    fresh pea & pasta broth, 10
    garden gazpacho, 9
    lamb-stuffed meatball, 18
    Mexican, with condiments, 15
    mushroom & vegetable, 10
    mussels, steamed, sesame-ginger, 12
    shrimp drop, 15
    tomatillo fish stew, 13

Soups (cont'd.)
    turkey hot pot, 18
    two-season Maltese, 12
    yellow squash, 9
Soy-lemon halibut, grilled, 59
Spaghetti squash, ground turkey sauce with, 81
Spices, happy, chicken with, 69
Spinach & tomatoes, chicken with, 70
Spinach crêpes, baked, 38
Spinach-rice crust, tuna pie with, 57
Spring harvest pasta salad, 24
Squash, spaghetti, ground turkey sauce with, 81
Squash, yellow, soup, 9
Steam-poached fish fillets or steaks, 61
Steam-poached whole fish, 61
Steeped chicken with basil dressing, 76
Steeped turkey with curry mayonnaise, 76
Stir-fried shrimp with Peking sauce, 62
Sugar vs. sugar substitutes, 104
Sweet pepper salsa, carrot &, 92
Sweet-sour flank steak, 85

T

Tacos, lettuce, 89
Tarragon-lemon vinaigrette, 31
Teriyaki fruit sauce, grilled tuna with, 51
Thighs, chicken, chutney-glazed, 79
Thyme, lemon &, grilled veal chops with, 95
Tofu salad sandwiches, deviled, 34
Tofulato
    banana, 105
    fresh berry, 105
    ginger or ginger-banana, 105
    vanilla, 105
Tofulato black & white, 105
Tomatillo fish stew, 13
Tomato & cucumber salad, 23
Tomato relish, Serbian, 54
Tomato salad, avocado-stuffed, 23
Tomato salsa, fresh, 92
Tomato sauce, Portuguese, 61
Tomatoes, spinach &, chicken with, 70
Tostada beef salad, 33
Tropical fruit gelato, 108
Tropical fruit salsa, 93
Trout, butterflied, with orange, 52
Trout, stuffed, calico, 52
Tuna, grilled, with teriyaki fruit sauce, 51
Tuna pie with spinach-rice crust, 57
Turkey
    barbecued, 80
    breast steaks, barbecued, 82
    ground, sauce with spaghetti squash, 81
    salad, cool curry, 32

Turkey (cont'd.)
    steeped, with curry mayonnaise, 76
    when to skin, 72
Turkey hot pot, 18
Turkey scaloppine with mushrooms, 82
Turkey scaloppine with peppers, 82
Two-grape chicken salad, 31
Two-season Maltese soup, 12

V

Vanilla frozen yogurt, 106
Vanilla tofulato, 105
Veal
    chops, grilled, with lemon & thyme, 95
    strips, mustard-glazed, 96
Veal sauté with peas, 95
Vegetable(s)
    crest, salmon with, 49
    herbed carrots & wild rice, 35
    julienne, omelet with, 43
    marinated asparagus with sesame, 33
    marinated sole with, 57
    matchstick zucchini, 36
    roasted new potatoes, 37
    sauté, beef &, 85
    seasoning, 36
    skewers, fish &, 54
    soup, mushroom &, 10
    zucchini bake, 35
Vegetable & bulgur stir-fry, 37
Vegetable burgers with peanut sauce, 39
Vegetables with lemon-dill dressing, 36
Vegetarian main dishes, 37–38
Vinaigrette dressing, cranberry, 25
Vinegar, chile, shrimp & jicama with, 29
Vitamins & minerals, 5

W

Watercress salad, hot beef &, 87
Wild rice, herbed carrots &, 35
Wine, light approach to, 88

Y

Yellow squash soup, 9
Yogurt, dressing salads with, 26
Yogurt-dill sauce, crusty fish with, 59
Yogurt salad, apple, 26
Yogurt soup, chicken-noodle, 16
Yugoslavian fish skewers, 54

Z

Zabaglione, champagne, oranges with, 103
Zucchini, matchstick, 36
Zucchini bake, 35
Zucchini omelets, 44

Metric Conversion Table

To change	To	Multiply by
ounces (oz.)	grams (g)	28
pounds (lbs.)	kilograms (kg)	0.45
teaspoons	milliliters (ml)	5
tablespoons	milliliters (ml)	15
fluid ounces (fl. oz.)	milliliters (ml)	30
cups	liters (l)	0.24
pints (pt.)	liters (l)	0.47
quarts (qt.)	liters (l)	0.95
gallons (gal.)	liters (l)	3.8
Fahrenheit temperature (°F)	Celsius temperature (°C)	⁵⁄₉ after subtracting 32

APR 2 6 2024